The Royal Court Theatre presents

Faith

by Meredith Oakes

D1638592

First performed at the **Royal Court Theatre Upstairs**,
West Street, 9 October 1997.

The Royal Court Theatre is financially assisted by the Royal
Borough of Kensington and Chelsea. Recipient of a grant from
the Theatre Restoration Fund & from the Foundation for Sport
& the Arts. The Royal Court's Play Development Programme
is funded by the A.S.K. Theater Projects. Supported by the National
Lottery through the Arts Council of England.
Royal Court Registered Charity number 231242.

FUNDED BY
LONDON
BOROUGHS
GRANTS
COMMITTEE

firstcall
TICKETS · 24 HOURS
0171 420 0100

Funded by
THE
ARTS
COUNCIL
OF ENGLAND

The English Stage Company at the Royal Court Theatre

The English Stage Company was formed to bring serious writing back to the stage. The first Artistic Director, George Devine, wanted to create a vital and popular theatre. He encouraged new writing that explored subjects drawn from contemporary life as well as pursuing European plays and forgotten classics. When John Osborne's **Look Back in Anger** was first produced in 1956, it forced British Theatre into the modern age. In addition to plays by 'angry young men', the international repertoire ranged from Brecht to Ionesco, by way of Jean-Paul Sartre, Marguerite Duras, Wedekind and Beckett.

The ambition was to discover new work which was challenging, innovative and also of the highest quality, underpinned by the desire to discover a contemporary style of presentation. Early Court writers included Arnold Wesker, John Arden, David Storey, Ann Jellicoe, N F Simpson and Edward Bond. They were followed by David Hare and Howard Brenton, Caryl Churchill, Timberlake Wertenbaker, Robert Holman and Jim Cartwright. Many of their plays are now regarded as modern classics.

Many established playwrights had their early plays produced in the Theatre Upstairs including Anne Devlin, Andrea Dunbar, Sarah Daniels, Jim Cartwright, Clare McIntyre, Winsome Pinnock, Martin Crimp and Phyllis Nagy. Since 1994 there has been a major season of plays by writers new to the Royal Court, many of them first plays, produced in association with the *Royal National Theatre Studio* with sponsorship from *The Jerwood Foundation*. The writers included Joe Penhall, Nick Grosso, Judy Upton, Sarah Kane, Michael Wynne, Judith Johnson, James Stock, Simon Block and Mark Ravenhill. In 1996-97 the Jerwood Foundation sponsored the Jerwood New Playwrights season, a series of six plays by Jez Butterworth, Martin McDonagh and Ayub Khan-Din (in the Theatre Downstairs), Mark Ravenhill, Tamantha Hammerschlag and Jess Walters (in the Theatre Upstairs).

Theatre Upstairs productions regularly transfer to the Theatre Downstairs, as with Ariel Dorfman's **Death and the Maiden**, Sebastian Barry's **The Steward of Christendom**, a co-production with *Out of Joint*, Martin McDonagh's **The Beauty Queen Of Leenane**, a co-production with Druid Theatre Company, and Ayub Khan-Din's **East is East**, a co-production with Tamasha Theatre Company. Some Theatre Upstairs productions have transferred to the West End, most recently with Kevin Elyot's **My Night With Reg** at the Criterion.

1992-1997 have been record-breaking years at the box-office with capacity houses for productions of **Death and the Maiden, Six Degrees of Separation, Oleanna, Hysteria, Cavalcaders, The Kitchen, The Queen & I, The Libertine, Simpatico, Mojo, The Steward of Christendom, The Beauty Queen of Leenane,** and **East is East.**

Death and the Maiden and **Six Degrees of Separation** won the Olivier Award for Best Play in 1992 and 1993 respectively. **Hysteria** won the 1994 Olivier Award for Best Comedy, and also the Writers' Guild Award for Best West End Play. **My Night with Reg** won the 1994 Writers' Guild Award for Best Fringe Play, the Evening Standard Award for Best Comedy, and the 1994 Olivier Award for Best Comedy. Jonathan Harvey won the 1994 Evening Standard Drama Award for Most Promising Playwright, for **Babies**. Sebastian Barry won the 1995 Writers' Guild Award for Best Fringe Play for **The Steward of Christendom** and also the 1995 Lloyds Private Banking Playwright of the Year Award. Jez Butterworth won the 1995 George Devine Award for Most Promising Playwright, the 1995 Writers' Guild New Writer of the Year, the Evening Standard Award for Most Promising Newcomer and the 1995 Olivier Award for Best Comedy for **Mojo**. Phyllis Nagy won the 1995 Writers' Guild Award for Best Regional Play for **Disappeared**. Martin McDonagh won the 1996 George Devine Award for Most Promising Playwright, the 1996 Writers' Guild Best Fringe Play Award, and the 1996 Evening Standard Drama Award for Most Promising Newcomer for **The Beauty Queen of Leenane**. Conor McPherson won the 1997 George Devine Award for Most Promising Playwright for **The Weir**. The Royal Court won the 1995 Prudential Award for the Theatre, and was the overall winner of the 1995 Prudential Award for the Arts for creativity, excellence, innovation and accessibility. The Royal Court won the 1995 Peter Brook Empty Space Award for innovation and excellence in theatre.

Now in its temporary homes, the Duke Of York's and Ambassadors Theatres, during the two-year refurbishment of its Sloane Square theatre, the Royal Court continues to present the best in new work. After four decades the company's aims remain consistent with those established by George Devine. The Royal Court is still a major focus in the country for the production of new work. Scores of plays first seen at the Royal Court are now part of the national and international dramatic repertoire.

Faith

by Meredith Oakes

Cast

Sergeant Toby Spiers	Howard Ward
Lance Corporal Adam Ziller	Karl Draper
Private Mick Pike	Jimmy Gallagher
Private Lee Finch	Callum Dixon
Sandra	Elizabeth Chadwick
Larry	John Sharian

Director	John Burgess
Designer	Anna Deamer
Lighting Designer	Hartley T A Kemp
Sound Design	Simon King
Assistant Director	Janette Smith
Assistant Designer	Jessica Curtis
Assistant Lighting Designer	Guy Hoare
Production Manager	Paul Handley
Company Stage Manager	Maris Sharp
Stage Managers	Pea Horsley
	Alexander Sims
Fight director	Terry Laing

The Ambassadors Theatre was re-designed by William Dudley.

The Royal Court would like to thank the following with this production: Wardrobe care by Persil and Comfort courtesy of Lever Brothers Ltd, refrigerators by Electrolux and Philips Major Appliances Ltd.; kettles for rehearsals by Morphy Richards; video for casting purposes by Hitachi; backstage coffee machine by West 9; furniture by Knoll International; freezer for backstage use supplied by Zanussi Ltd 'Now that's a good idea.' Hair styling by Carole at Moreno, 2 Holbein Place, Sloane Square 0171-730-0211; Closed circuit TV cameras and monitors by Mitsubishi UK Ltd. Natural spring water from Aqua Cool, 12 Waterside Way, London SW17 0XH, tel. 0181-947 5666. Overhead projector from W.H. Smith; Sanyo U.K for the backstage microwave; Watford Palace Theatre.

Meredith Oakes (writer)
For the Royal Court: The Editing Process. Other theatre includes: The Neighbour (RNT); Mind the Gap (Hampstead Theatre). Opera libretti include: The Triumph of Beauty and Deceit (Channel 4); Jump into my Sack (Mecklenburg Opera).
Translations include: Miss Julie (Young Vic); Elizabeth II (Gate Theatre); The New Menoza (Gate Theatre & Edinburgh Festival).
Television includes: Prime Suspect IV.

John Burgess (director)
Theatre includes: Present Laughter (Aarhus Theatre, Denmark); When Did You Last See My Mother? (BAC); The School for Scandal (English Touring Theatre); Rupert Street Lonely Hearts Club (Donmar Warehouse & Criterion Theatre); Edward II (Stadttheater, Berne); The Neighbour, When We Were Women, Neaptide, The Garden of England, Sunday Morning, True Dare Kiss, Command or Promise, Antigone, The Prince of Homburg, Serjeant Musgrave's Dance (RNT); Hurricane Roses, Street Trash, What Country, The Way South, Bow Down, Weights and Measures, Black Poppies, Macbeth, Travelling Time, The Freud Scenario, The Women, Carrington, Bit A' Business (RNT Studio); Black Poppies (Theatre Royal, Stratford East); Schism in England, When We Were Women (Edinburgh Festival); The Way South (Bush Theatre); Down By the Greenwood Side / Bow Down (Queen Elizabeth Hall); Richard III (National Theatre of Iceland); Black Man's Burden, One Fine Day, Treetops, One Third of the Kingdom, One is One (Riverside Studios); Red Earth (ICA). Repertory in Ipswich, Leeds, Coventry, Birmingham & Colchester.
Television includes: Black Poppies.

Elizabeth Chadwick
Theatre includes: Summer Begins (Donmar Warehouse); When We Are Married (Chichester Festival & Savoy); The Life of Stuff (Donmar Warehouse); Clandestine Marriage (Queen's); Somewhere (Springboards Festival, RNT & Liverpool Playhouse); Romeo and Juliet (Contact Theatre); Dreams of Anne Frank (Polka Theatre); The Three Musketeers (Sheffield Crucible); The Party's Over (Theatre Royal, Northampton); The Lion, The Witch and The Wardrobe (Westminster Theatre).

Television includes: Eastenders, Peak Practice, The Vet, Paris, Fun With Wigs.

Anna Deamer (designer)
Theatre includes: A Midsummer Night's Dream (Fellow's Gardens, Cambridge); Second Thoughts (London Bubble); The Belle of Belfast City (Orange Tree); Uncle Vanya (Theatre Museum).
Television includes: (as Production Designer) I Just Want to Kiss You, The Bill, Peter York's 80's, Divine Magic: Angels, British Slaves, (as Art Director) Tom Jones, The Vanishing Man, Roger, Roger, Beck, Killing Me Softly, For Valour.
Trained in fine art at Wimbledon School of Art, and theatre design at Motley Theatre Design Course. Stage 1 prizewinner for the Linbury Prize for Stage Design.

Callum Dixon
For the Royal Court: Mojo, Young Writers' Festival.
Other theatre includes: The Wind in the Willows, Somewhere, The Recruiting Officer, Rosencrantz and Guildenstern Are Dead (RNT); Edward II, Richard III, Two Shakespearian Actors, Bright and Bold Design (RSC); Accrington Pals, Mowgli's Jungle (Octagon Theatre, Bolton); All I Want to Be is An Ugly Sister (Lilian Baylis Theatre); Waiting at the Water's Edge (Bush Theatre); Macbeth (British Actors' Co UK tour); Voytex (RNT Studio); Deadwood (Watermill Theatre).
Television includes: The Queen's Nose, The Bill, The Knock III, The Tomorrow People, Hetty Wainthrop Investigates.
Film includes: Waterlands.
Radio includes: The Wolfgang Chase.

Karl Draper
For the Royal Court: Uganda, Babies.
Other theatre includes: Boom Bang A Bang (Bush Theatre); Somewhere (RNT); Coyote Ugly (Old Red Lion); The Hatchet Man (D.O.C.); The Millionairess (The Rose, Fulham); Arki-types (Etcetera Theatre); Song of Myself (Greenwich Theatre).
Television includes: Mosley, Staying Alive 1 & 2, Out of the Blue, Kavanagh QC, The Bill, Oliver's Travels, Grushko.

Jimmy Gallagher
Theatre includes: The Ale House (Liverpool Everyman); Hoover Bag (Young Vic Studio); Heroes, Waiting For Godot, The Blue Angel

All Flesh is Grass (Liverpool Playhouse); Indigo, The Taming of the Shrew (RSC Stratford, Newcastle, & world tour); Fen (RSC Stratford Festival); Reynard Fox (RSC Festival, Newcastle); Revenger's Tragedy, Hyde Park, Merchant of Venice, Bite of the Night (RSC Barbican); Titus Andronicus (RSC, European tour); The Plough and the Stars (Abbey, Dublin).

Television includes: Scully, Come On And Down Out, Safe, The Bill, Kidney Theft, Rich Deceiver.

Film includes: Priest.

Hartley T A Kemp (lighting designer)
Theatre includes: Rosmersholm, Seascape with Sharks and Dancer (Southwark Playhouse); Bloody Poetry (Cardiff); When Did You Last See My Mother?, Baby Jean, High Germany (BAC); The Little Mermaid, The Snow Queen (Edinburgh & the Chelsea Centre); Jabberwocky (Edinburgh); A Week with Tony (Finborough); Stealing, Untrue Stories (New End Theatre); Shakespeare for Breakfast (Edinburgh & Singapore); Dorlan (Arts Theatre); Jesus Christ - Superstar (Theatre Royal, Hanley); Assassins, Sweet Lorraine (Old Fire Station, Oxford); The Happy Prince (UK tour).
Opera includes: Iris (Holland Park Opera); Carmen (Castle Ward Opera); Die Fledermaus (Chichester Festival & UK tour); The Promise (Queen Elizabeth Hall & Staines); The Marriage of Figaro (Queen Elizabeth Hall & UK tour).
Assistant lighting design includes: The Herbal Bed (RSC); Happy Days (Almeida); Smokey Joe's Cafe (Prince of Wales); Sunset Boulevard (Frankfurt).
Re-light credits include: Carcalla Dance Theatre (Peacock Theatre, London, Beirut, Damascus, Dubai); La Boheme, Madame Butterfly (Crystal Clear Opera).
Also programmes and runs C venues at the Edinburgh Festival.

Simon King (sound designer)
For the Royal Court: The Call, Drinking, Smoking and Tokeing, Cockroach Who?, Where the Devils Dwell.
Other theatre includes: Maria Friedman (Hilton); Scenofest (Central St Martin's College of Art & Design); 3 Ms Behaving (Tricycle Theatre); Cinderella (AMP Piccadilly).
Deputy Head of Sound at the Royal Court.

John Sharian
For the Royal Court: The One You Love.
Other theatre includes: Lone Stars and PVT Wars, The Life and Death of a Buffalo Soldier, The Hairy Ape (Bristol Old Vic); Macbeth, View From the Bridge (York Theatre Royal); A Lie of the Mind (BAC); Laundry Room at the Hotel Madrid (Gate Theatre); Small Craft Warnings (Manchester Library); Hamlet (Shaw Theatre); Entertaining Mr Sloane, Who's Afraid of Virginia Woolf, Safe Sex, The Importance of Being Earnest, Curse of the Starving Class, A Streetcar Named Desire (New Ehrlich Theatre, USA); As You Like it, American Buffalo, Servant of Two Masters, Getting Out (Kenyon Festival, USA); No End of Blame, The Castle (Playwrights' Platform, USA); Two For the Seesaw, Harvey, Fifth of July (Tufts Arena Stage, USA); Macbeth (American Repertory Theatre); Baal, The Taming of the Shrew (Boston Stage Company).
Television includes: Crocodile Shoes, Dead Men's Tales, Red Dwarf, Where in the World is Carmen Sandiego?
Film includes: Saving Private Ryan, Lost in Space, Fifth Element, Death Machine, Two Sane Men.

Howard Ward
For the Royal Court: Attempts on Her Life, Pale Horse.
Other theatre includes: Johnny On the Spot, Wind in the Willows, Mountain Giants, Macbeth, Night of the Iguana (RNT); All's Well that Ends Well, As You Like It, The Two Noble Kinsmen, The Fair Maid of the West, The Balcony, The Triumph of the Egg, The Great White Hope, Speculators (RSC); Chicago (Leicester Haymarket); The Odd Couple, The Daughter-in-Law, All My Sons (Thorndike); Death of a Salesman (Nottingham); Little Shop of Horrors, Flashpoint, Merrily We Roll Along (Library Theatre, Manchester); Stags and Hens (York); Mother Courage (Theatre Foundry); One Big Blow (Dukes Theatre, Lancaster).
Television includes: The Bill, Insiders, Eastenders, Story Store, Jake's Progress, Peak Practice, Between the Lines, London's Burning, Minder, All Creatures Great and Small, Brookside, The Practice, Bust, Albion Market, Upline.
Radio includes: Let's Move, Survival, Sandra and the Seagulls, The Taxman (director), The Last Dare (director).

GRANADA

GRANADA GROUP PLC

Message from The Chairman, Development Board

Dear Royal Court Supporter,

The Royal Court Theatre has a track record of success; I am associated with it because it is uniquely placed to take advantage of the current climate of optimism, energy and innovation.

Our plans for the transformed theatre in Sloane Square include the latest stage technology, a café bar and improved audience facilities enabling us to anticipate the latest in contemporary drama whilst at the same time the refurbished building will bear testimony to our past successes.

I invite you to become part of these exciting plans.

Gerry Robinson
Chairman, Granada Group Plc

We Need Your Support

The Royal Court Theatre, Sloane Square, was built in 1888 and is the longest-established theatre in England with the dedicated aim of producing new plays. We were thrilled to be awarded £16.2 million in September 1995 - from the National Lottery through the Arts Council of England - towards the complete renovation and restoration of our 100-year old home. This award has provided us with a unique opportunity to redevelop this beautiful theatre and building work is already underway at the Sloane Square site. However, in order to receive the full Lottery award, the Royal Court must raise almost £6 million itself as partnership funding towards the capital project.

The support of individuals, companies, charitable trusts and foundations is of vital importance to the realisation of the redevelopment of the Royal Court Theatre and we are very grateful to those who have already made a major contribution:

BSkyB Ltd
Double O Charity
Granada Group Plc
News International Plc
Pathé
Peter Jones
Quercus Charitable Trust
The Trusthouse Charitable Foundation

The *Stage Hands Appeal* was launched with the aim of raising over £500,000 from audience members and the general public, towards our £6 million target.

So far the appeal has met with great success and we are grateful to our many supporters who have so generously donated to the appeal. However, we still have some way to go to reach our goal and each donation keeps the building work at Sloane Square moving forward; for example a donation of £20 pays for 40 bricks, a donation of £50 pays for cedar panelling for the auditorium and a donation of £100 pays for two square meters of reclaimed timber flooring.

If you would like to help, please complete the donation form enclosed in this playtext (additional forms are available from the Box Office) and return it to: Development Office, Royal Court Theatre, St. Martin's Lane, London WC2N 4BG.

For more information please contact the Development Office on 0171 930 4253.

Royal Court Theatre Capital Appeal... Royal Court Theatre Capital Appeal... Royal Court Theatre Capital Appeal...

How the Royal Court is brought to you

The Royal Court (English Stage Company Ltd) is supported financially by a wide range of private companies and public bodies and earns the remainder of its income from the Box Office and its own trading activities. The company receives its principal funding from the Arts Council of England, which has supported the Court since 1956. The Royal Borough of Kensington & Chelsea gives an annual grant to the Royal Court Young People's Theatre and the London Boroughs Grants Committee contributes to the cost of productions in the Theatre Upstairs.

Other parts of the company's activities are made possible by sponsorship and private foundation support. 1993 saw the start of our association with the Audrey Skirball-Kenis Theatre of Los Angeles, which is funding a Playwrights Programme at the Royal Court, and 1997 marks the third Jerwood Foundation Jerwood New Playwrights series, supporting the production of new plays by young writers.

We are grateful to all our supporters for their vital and on-going commitment.

TRUSTS AND FOUNDATIONS
The Baring Foundation
The Campden Charities
John Cass's Foundation
The Chase Charity
The Esmeé Fairbairn
 Charitable Trust
The Robert Gavron
 Charitable Trust
Paul Hamlyn Foundation
The Jerwood Foundation
The John Lyons' Charity
The Mercers' Charitable
 Foundation
The Prince's Trust
Peggy Ramsay Foundation
The Rayne Foundation
The Lord Sainsbury
 Foundation for Sport & the Arts
The Wates Foundation

SPONSORS
AT&T
Barclays Bank
Hugo Boss
The Granada Group Plc
Marks & Spencer Plc
The New Yorker

PRIVATE SUBSCRIBERS
Patrons
Advanpress
Associated Newspapers Ltd
Sir Christopher Bland
Bunzl Plc
Chubb Insurance Company of
 Europe
Citigate Communications
Criterion Productions Plc
Dibb Lupton Alsop
Greg Dyke
Homevale Ltd
Laporte Plc
Lazard Brothers & Co. Ltd
Lex Service Plc
Patricia Marmont
Barbara Minto
The Mirror Group Plc
New Penny Productions Ltd
Noel Gay Artists/Hamilton Asper
 Management
A T Poeton & Son Ltd
Greville Poke
Richard Pulford
Sir George Russell
The Simkins Partnership
Simons Muirhead and
 Burton
Richard Wilson

Benefactors
Mr & Mrs Gerry Acher
Bill Andrewes
Elaine Attias
Angela Bernstein
Jeremy Bond
Katie Bradford
Julia Brodie
Julian Brookstone
Guy Chapman
Yuen-Wei Chew
Carole & Neville Conrad
Conway van Gelder
Coppard Fletcher & Co.
Lisa Crawford Irwin
Curtis Brown Ltd
Robyn Durie
Gill Fitzhugh
Kim Fletcher & Sarah Sands
Winston Fletcher
Claire & William Frankel
Nicholas A Fraser
Norman Gerard
Henny Gestetner OBE
Jules Goddard

Carolyn Goldbart
Rocky Gottlieb
Stephen Gottlieb
Frank & Judy Grace
Jan Harris
Angela Heylin
Andre Hoffman
Chris Hopson
Juliet Horsman
Trevor Ingman
Institute of Practitioners
 in Advertising
International Creative
 Management
Peter Jones
Thomas & Nancy Kemeny
Sahra Lese
Judy Lever
Lady Lever
Sally Margulies
Sir Alan and Lady Moses
The Hon. Mrs A. Montagu
Pat Morton
Paul Oppenheimer
Michael Orr
Sir Eric Parker
Lynne Pemberton
Carol Rayman
Penny Reed
Angharad Rees
B J & Rosemary Reynolds
John Sandoe (Books) Ltd
Scott Tallon Walker
Nicholas Selmes
David & Patricia Smalley
Sue Stapely
Dr Gordon Taylor
A P Thompson
Tomkins Plc
Elizabeth Tyson
A P Watt Ltd
Nick Wilkinson

AMERICAN FRIENDS
Patrons
Miriam Blenstock
Tina Brown
Caroline Graham
Richard & Marcia Grand
Edwin & Lola Jaffe
Ann & Mick Jones
Maurie Perl
Rhonda Sherman

Members
Monica Gerard-Sharp
Linda S. Lese
Yasmine Lever
Gertrude Oothout
Leila Maw Strauss
Enid W. Morse
Mr & Mrs Frederick Rose
Mrs Paul Soros

Autumn at the Royal Court

Theatre Downstairs
St Martin's Lane WC2

From 17 September
until 18 October

The Royal Court and Out of Joint present

BLUE HEART
by Caryl Churchill
directed by Max Stafford-Clark

From 23 October
FAIRGAME
by Rebecca Prichard
A free adaptation of GAMES IN
THE BACKYARD by Edna Mazya
directed by Roxana Silbert

From 19 November
*The Royal Court and Theatre de
Complicite in association with the
French Theatre Season and
sponsored by Barclays as part of
Barclays New Stages - Staging the New*

THE CHAIRS
by Eugène Ionesco
Translated by Martin Crimp
Directed by Simon McBurney

Theatre Upstairs
West St. WC2

18 November - 20 December
NEW EUROPEAN WRITING SEASON

*produced by the Royal Court
International Department, in
association with the British Council*

One More Wasted Year
by Christophe Pellet

Bazaar
by David Planell

Stranger's House
by Dea Loher

Further details available
from the box office

Rehearsed Readings

Four outstanding new French plays
in translation from 19-22 November
at 7.00pm each evening
Four new German comedies in
translation from 3-6 December at
7.00pm each evening

BOX OFFICE 0171 565 5000

Every Friendship is give and take

You give us £20 each year a a one-off initial joining fee of £25 and we give you:

*Two top price tickets for
every production in the
Theatre Downstairs for only
£5 each

*Two top price tickets for
every production in the
Theatre Upstairs for only
£5 each

*Priority booking for all
productions at the Royal Cou

*Free tickets to selected
Royal Court readings and
other special events

*You will also receive a
newsletter including articles
from writers, directors and
other artists working at the
Royal Court, and special
offers for other theatres
and arts events

AFTER JOINING YOU WILL ONLY HAVE TO PURCHASE TWO TICKET IN THE THEATRE DOWNSTAIRS A YOU WILL HAVE ALREADY SAVED £

TO JOIN SIMPLY COMPLETE THE
FORM AVAILABLE AT THE
BOX OFFICE COUNTER

ALSO PUBLISHED BY OBERON BOOKS:

Meredith Oakes

THE EDITING PROCESS

Price: £5.99

Paperback: 74pp – ISBN 1 870259 46 7

"If you want to catch the spirit of 1990's England, you may discover it distilled in Meredith Oakes' dry new satire."

The Evening Standard

Meredith Oakes' comedy of fragile values in the media will not restore your faith in human nature, but it is guaranteed to help you get on in publishing without really succeeding. First performed at The Royal Court in 1995, directed by Stephen Daldry.

Meredith Oakes

THE NEIGHBOUR

Price: £5.99

Paberback: 64pp – ISBN 1 870259 31 9

"Very sharp and funny while laying bare a sad sense of waste and despair."

The Independent

Two young men living on a council estate suddenly become enemies, invoking destructive forces beyond their control. The community takes sides like spectators cheering from a grandstand. First performed at the Royal National Theatre Springboard Season (Cottesloe) in 1992.

FAITH

by Meredith Oakes

OBERON BOOKS
LONDON

First published in 1997 by Oberon Books Ltd
(incorporating Absolute Classics),
521 Caledonian Road, London, N7 9RH.
Tel: 0171 607 3637 / Fax: 0171 607 3629

British Library Cataloguing-in-Publication Data
A catalogue record for this book is available from the British Library.

ISBN 1 870259 80 7

Front cover design: P A News

Series design: Andrzej Klimowski

Cover typography: Richard Doust

Printed in Great Britain by Arrowhead Books, Reading

Characters

SERGEANT TOBY SPIERS, 39

LANCE CORPORAL ADAM ZILLER, 28

PRIVATE MICK PIKE, 20

PRIVATE LEE FINCH, 19

SANDRA, 30s

LARRY, American, 30

Setting: A remote island farmhouse at a time of war, 1982

FIRST SECTION

Kitchen of the house lived in by the manager of the farm. Sink full of mugs etc. Bright day, winter.

TOBY, ADAM.

TOBY: If you've something to say to me, say it. (*Silence.*) For better or worse, you're an influence. That's to your credit, corporal. You've become an influence thanks to your achievements. I grant you that. (*Silence.*) Did you speak. Did I hear you speak. (*Silence.*) But influence carries with it responsibility. Doesn't it, corporal. (*Silence.*) I could have you on a charge! Don't think I wouldn't. (*Silence.*) It's not that I like it. You think I like it. What boots are those. (*Silence.*) Where did you get those boots, did you get those boots last night, did you. (*Silence.*) All I'm saying is, what I do, I do for your good. Because I have a perspective. (*Silence.*) I'm looking after you. That's all I'm trying to do, is look after you.

ADAM: Cunt.

ADAM off. TOBY alone.

TOBY: Cunt he says. Quite a definite observation. Cunt he says... The moment she appeared. The moment she appeared I had to press the button to open the doors...

SANDRA enters and sees the mugs in the sink.

SANDRA: I'm not washing those.

TOBY: No love, you leave those.

SANDRA: I'm not washing those.

TOBY: You leave them.

SANDRA: I'm definitely not washing those. (*She runs water in the sink, starts washing mugs.*) The moment I step outside that door. Here comes the skeleton, says one. Like fucking a pair of chopsticks, says another. I'm only going out to empty the slops. I'm not a fucking chorus line. What do they want. A fucking floorshow. The dog runs up and jumps on me. Scratch her tit, says one. Oh yes, we're living life to the full out there. Scratch her tit. Are you going to speak to them.

TOBY: Yes all right love.

SANDRA: You said to me that you were going to speak to them.

TOBY: Yes love.

SANDRA: Anyway. If I'm such a skeleton. How come I've got tits.

ADAM enters.

TOBY: Shut the door corporal.

ADAM: –

TOBY: It's cold with that door open, shut the door.

ADAM: Where am I going to put him.

TOBY: Have you forgotten what a door is, corporal.

ADAM: (*Knocks on the table.*) Hullo.

TOBY: (*Frightened, but determined to continue.*) Forgotten what a door is. You've been out of doors too long, corporal, you've forgotten what a house is.

ADAM: Where am I going to put him.

TOBY: Shut the door.

ADAM: Cunt.

ADAM off, leaving the door open.

SANDRA: That's not very nice. He's not very nice.

TOBY: (*Shutting the door.*) Yes sergeant. I'll shut the do/
sergeant.

SANDRA: I'm keeping well away from him.

TOBY: You do that, love.

SANDRA: Keep my distance from him.

TOBY: You do that.

SANDRA: Sooner him and his kind are out of here.

TOBY: Soon enough, love. We'll be out of here soon
enough.

SANDRA: No-one in my son's room all right.

TOBY: There's people kipping up and down the house.

SANDRA: I'm not having anyone go up in my son's room.
That's my one remaining area of sanity.

TOBY: Yes I can see how special that is, love.

SANDRA: Eh.

TOBY: No-one in your son's room, I promised you didn't I.

SANDRA: Doesn't like you, does he.

TOBY: What makes you say that.

SANDRA: Well he doesn't, does he.

TOBY: I'm not answerable to you, love.

SANDRA: I never said you was.

TOBY: My feet.

SANDRA: Eh.

TOBY: If it hadn't been for my feet. Apart from my feet,
Sandra, I'm fitter now than what I've ever been. I was
carrying my own weight again, Sandra. The night we set

off to come over here, I was carrying my own weight again. One lad fell in a ditch. He was carrying so much weight he broke his back. I had no problem with the weight. I had a problem with the boots. Someone's idea of a joke our fucking boots. Someone's idea of a bargain. I took off my boots. In my sock I found the nail of my big toe. My feet were blue, with a line of red round the edges. The orderly takes one look, he says to me, You're fortunate your nail fell off and not your toes, he says. Where do you think you're off to, he says, you're not going off up the mountain with those feet. Yes I am, I say. Why don't I cut them off right now, he says, if I hear any more about you going off up the mountain, that's what I'm going to do, cut them off, save myself the trouble later on.

SANDRA: What's his name.

TOBY: Who.

SANDRA: Rude bugger.

TOBY: Angry twenty-four hours a day, the lance corporal. (*Laughs.*) Angry with me for being not as angry as he is.

SANDRA: Walks in here as if he owns it.

TOBY: And yet, Sandra. All the time, I'm looking after them.

SANDRA: And what do you do. You do nothing.

TOBY: I don't get emotional see, I don't get angry, there's too much at stake to get angry. It weakens me if I get angry, Sandra. Some people, it strengthens. The lance corporal thrives on getting angry. This makes him useful in certain situations. I'm useful in other situations.

SANDRA: I'm keeping well away from him. What's his name.

TOBY: Lance corporal Ziller. The other lads call him God.

SANDRA: Eh?

TOBY: Godzilla.

ADAM and MICK bring LARRY in, beaten up. MICK also brings some mugs which he leaves by the sink.

TOBY: Not in here, corporal.

SANDRA: My God what is this.

TOBY: I never said you could bring him in here.

SANDRA: What is this.

TOBY: Christ!

SANDRA: I'm not having that in here.

TOBY: The lady would prefer you not to bring the gentleman in here.

SANDRA: Fuck off out of here, put him in the shed with the rest of them.

ADAM: Shut your face love.

ADAM and MICK off, leaving LARRY in the kitchen.

SANDRA: (*To TOBY.*) You hear what he said to me? He'd better not say that again. (*Running off after ADAM.*) You come here and say that again!

TOBY: ... The moment she appeared I had to press the button to open the doors. Then I had to nip inside the lift and hold the Door Open button pressed down while she and the brass got in... (*To LARRY.*) Come on, you're all right. (*Clicks his fingers.*) Hear that? (*Clicks his fingers.*) Come on. You can hear that. Look, I saw what happened. They hardly touched you. I put a stop to it, didn't I. Soon as they started, I put a stop to it. You try talking about this, you won't get a hearing. You'll do yourself no good by making an issue out of this. Because I stopped it. Straight away. They as good as never touched you. If you want to do yourself some good. I tell you what you should talk about. Minefields you should talk about. Disposition of enemy troops you should talk about. Do us both a bit of good you can. They'd be pleased with me, and I'd be pleased with you. It's not betrayal. Anything you can tell me that helps get this war over quicker and easier is not betrayal. Nobody wants any more fighting and killing than is strictly necessary. Nobody wants that. Do they. You're a rational man. We can do with that. A bit of rationality...

LEE enters, with a tray full of mugs which he leaves by the sink.

LEE: Sarge.

TOBY: This gentleman and I are conversing.

LEE: He's out cold sarge.

TOBY: This gentleman and I are having a chat.

LEE: Yes sarge. When they bring us the stuff sarge. When do you think it will be sarge.

TOBY: I told you Finch I don't know.

LEE: We'll be dead before they bring that stuff, sitting here in the middle of nowhere, one rocket we're history.

TOBY: What do you want Finch.

LEE: Yes well when they bring the stuff it's my turn, that's all I'm saying. Like I said to you, last time, Mick got the last of the Mars Bars and I had a Yorkie. And the time before that, same thing, he got the last of the Mars Bars and I finished up with the Yorkie.

TOBY: My goodness did you Finch.

LEE: Yes I did sarge.

TOBY: I see, Finch. Yes I see. Finch. Why are you telling me this?

LEE: Well can't you see, sarge. Because this time, I want a Mars, is why.

TOBY: What am I going to do about it, Finch.

LEE: What you should do.

TOBY: Yes.

LEE: What you should do. When they drop them. You should take all of them sarge.

TOBY: All of the chocolate bars.

LEE: Yes sarge. And cut them up in pieces all the same, exactly the same, and give them out. That's what you should always do.

TOBY: That seems like the adult solution yes.

LEE: I can't understand why no-one's thought of it.

TOBY: How could they, Finch, they lack your vision.

LEE: How are the feet sarge.

TOBY: You did well last night, I hear.

LEE: Done my duty sarge.

TOBY: You didn't let me down.

LEE: How are the feet.

TOBY: My fucking feet.

LEE: How are they sarge.

TOBY: Getting there, Finch, getting there. I'm looking after them Finch.

LEE: That's good, sarge.

TOBY: It's not as if I could have achieved anything. If I'd have been up there.

LEE: Never say that, sarge.

TOBY: No I couldn't Finch. I'd just have been in the way.

LEE: Never say that. There was a lot of them dead round the rocks up there this morning sarge.

TOBY: Yes I believe so.

LEE: Godzilla, sarge, you should have seen him.

TOBY: Yes I believe he pulled Jennings out of the line of fire.

LEE: Jennings sat up sarge. I thought he was alive. Godzilla pushed him flat again, he just sat up again.

TOBY: How do you mean he sat up again.

LEE: Sat up. Bolt upright. Dead.

TOBY: Must have been something the matter with him, Finch.

LEE: Yes sarge.

TOBY: Did you see that, did you.

LEE: Yes sarge.

TOBY: Yes well you and your prisoners Finch, you haven't half given me a headache, arsing round up there causing people to surrender, we've got more fucking prisoners than we've got men.

LEE: When I saw that fucking white flag, I couldn't have been more surprised if I'd have seen a fucking yeti.

TOBY: No yeti would live here Finch, it's not that hospitable.

LEE: You know what they say, sarge, expect the unexpected. The greatest shock sarge. The greatest shock is when the expected is what actually happens. You've thought of it before. That is what kills you. Things you were only used to having in your mind, like loading your weapon while being shot at for instance, these things are actually happening, this is why it seems like a dream. I hadn't got the foggiest where anybody was half the time, round those rocks, no knowing what I was firing at, no notion of who's firing at me, and I tripped over something, it's a dead man with smoke pouring out of his jacket, like his jacket is hollow, it was fucking mad up there sarge.

TOBY: Was it Finch.

LEE: It was absolute chaos up there.

TOBY: I doubt that, Finch.

LEE: You didn't see what it was like sarge.

TOBY: Chaos was it.

LEE: Yes sarge.

TOBY: That's your opinion, is it.

LEE: Yes sarge.

TOBY: How long have you been with us, Finch?

LEE: Two years, sarge.

TOBY: Long time.

LEE: I wouldn't say that sarge.

TOBY: Long enough for you to have an opinion, would you say.

LEE: No sarge.

TOBY: No sarge. When you've served as many hours as I have days, Finch, then you can have an opinion.

LEE: Yes sarge.

TOBY: If it was chaos, Finch, the victor could have been anyone.

LEE: Yes, sarge.

TOBY: But it wasn't anyone, it was us.

LEE: Yes sarge.

TOBY: Therefore it wasn't chaos. Was it.

LEE: Eh.

TOBY: Superiority is organization, Finch. What is the most superior species on earth. Man. Man is the most highly organized, i.e. the most superior. The British fighting man is the most highly organized of men.

LEE: Yes sarge.

TOBY: That's why we won.

LEE: Yes sarge.

TOBY: (*Indicating LARRY.*) Watch him.

LEE: I'll have a chat with him sarge.

TOBY off. LEE sits listening to music on his cassette player with headphones. LARRY remains seated. ADAM looks in. Withdraws. Sneaks in with a camera, soon joined by MICK. ADAM is secretly photographing LEE from behind.

ADAM: Eh Finch. (*LEE doesn't hear. MICK goes up to him, ADAM too, still taking pictures.*)

MICK: Finch!

LEE: (*Takes headphones off.*) Eh?

MICK: Something crawling on you.

LEE: (*Turns music off.*) Where?

MICK: (*Indicates.*) Look.

LEE discovers a severed hand tucked in the back of his sweater or in one of his sleeve pockets, the fingers placed as if trying to climb out.

LEE: Get it off me.

MICK: (*Pointing at LEE, laughing.*) Your face man! (*To ADAM.*) His face!

ADAM: (*Taking photographs.*) Never mind his face what about his hand.

LEE: You fucking cunts. Get it off me.

ADAM: I'm not touching that, I don't know where it's been.

LEE: (*To MICK.*) Whose is it, is it yours?

MICK: (*Looking at his hands.*) No I got mine here mate.

LEE: (*Trying to bring himself to take the hand off.*) I can't. It's so sad.

The others roar with laughter.

ADAM: It's so sad.

MICK: It is, Lee, it is. So sad.

LEE: You laugh, you laugh! How would you like it if that was you! (*He indicates the hand. The others laugh.*) He's dead isn't he, what more do you want. If you knew what fools you look like, laughing at a dead man. You're laughing in silence. You can't hear it, that's all. I'd rather be mates with wasps. I'd rather be mates with flies.

They're still laughing. LEE gets a tea towel, lifts the hand off and throws it furiously at MICK, who catches it.

MICK: Why am I here. Look at the skin on it. Look at the hairs. Urgh. Thank Christ I'm not a doctor. (*He throws the hand at ADAM, who's photographing him.*) David Bailey. Thinks he's David Bailey.

ADAM: With your disgusting features in my lens. I don't think so.

MICK: What do you want. Marie. (*He mimes her.*)

ADAM: Marie Helvin is the most beautiful woman in the world.

MICK: We know. You told us. The little hands. The beautiful skin like a peach. Old though isn't she. Twenty-what. Face it, Ziller, I'm ten years younger.

LEE: I'd give her one.

MICK: Really. Would you.

LEE: Yes laugh, you laugh. You're not fit to shine her shoes.

MICK: It wouldn't be shining her shoes though, would it, polishing her zimmer frame is what it would be...

ADAM: (*Smashes MICK and then speaks exactly in his former tone.*) Marie Helvin is the most beautiful woman in the world.

MICK: Yes you're right. The most beautiful woman in the world. Yes she is.

ADAM: Where's Tobes.

MICK: Bit old though.

LEE: I come in here, he's talking to that man there.

ADAM: What man where.

LEE: I say to him, sarge, he's out cold. We're having a conversation, he says, we're having a chat.

MICK: Only person that'll talk to him.

ADAM: Cunt.

LEE: I didn't know where to look, I didn't know where to put myself.

MICK: Tobes the feet.

ADAM: If he says one word more about his feet. Just one more word. I'll kill the cunt. Sitting there holding them out to dry. Putting baby powder on them. Know what he says to me. I'm treating my feet as if they were my babies, he says. I say what. Fiddling with them, Tobes.

MICK: The doctor. Going to the doctor with his feet.

ADAM: I never went to the doctor with my feet. Open sores I've got on my feet the size of strawberries. I never went to the doctor.

MICK: The trouble with Tobes, he's been in the military so long, he thought he was safe in the military.

LEE: Job for life yeah.

MICK: Pension to look forward to.

LEE: He joined up for the security.

MICK: His career as a soldier has been ruined by war.

LEE: He keeps going on at me.

MICK: But he's got so much to go on about, hasn't he, cos not everyone has got a wife who's practically completed a –

ALL THREE: Wine tasting course.

MICK: And she's so houseproud –

LEE: You have to leave your shoes by the front door.

MICK: And they've got a lovely –

ALL THREE: Spanish style coffee table.

ADAM: Cunt.

MICK: Who's that woman.

ADAM: A woman of the island.

LEE: What a head case.

MICK: No thanks.

LEE: Eh.

MICK: Head. No thanks.

LEE: Oh... No. Maybe not.

MICK: You're disgusting.

LEE: Maybe not.

MICK: Makes brew for him in a union jack mug.

ADAM: Powerful erotic signal.

LEE: Nothing else for them to do, is there. They've no television.

MICK: They're primitive people. It's like going back in time to 1950.

LEE: They've got no roads. They've got horses.

ADAM: Terrifying animals. Violent. Unpredictable.

MICK: Terrifying.

ADAM: They're throwbacks.

MICK: They're all mentally strange, perverts and weird the lot of them.

LEE: You'll fit right in then Mick.

MICK: Look who's talking. I'm not the one blew a man in half with a rocket.

ADAM: Did he.

MICK: You should have seen it. It was mental. The poor cunt's legs dropped straight down the rocks, the top half goes flying up in the sky like a pop-up toaster.

ADAM: Oh how I wish I'd been there.

MICK: Bonkers though, isn't it.

ADAM: That's a bit evil, Finch.

MICK: That's twenty grand's worth.

LEE: I lost my temper.

ADAM: You're too sensitive.

LEE: (*Indicates LARRY.*) What's up with him then?

ADAM: Who.

LEE: I wondered what happened, that's all.

TOBY enters.

TOBY: You're going to have to get on the radio, corporal, ask what they want us to do with him.

ADAM: Am I sarge.

TOBY: You don't say that. Am I, sarge. You don't say that.

ADAM: Don't I sarge.

ADAM off.

TOBY: You should get some kip, Pike.

MICK: Can't sleep sarge, I'll sleep tonight.

TOBY: Are you looking forward to that are you.

MICK: Certainly am.

TOBY: Like it here, do you.

MICK: Oh sarge this was a master stroke. Wind's like a knife out there.

TOBY: So you're going to kip tonight, are you.

MICK: First night's kip in days.

TOBY: Who says you'll still be here tonight.

MICK: You did sarge.

TOBY: You must be mistaken Pike. They want you back up again tonight.

LEE: We've just come down sarge.

TOBY: Well tonight you're going back up again.

LEE: You might have said before sarge.

TOBY: I couldn't face the look in your eyes Finch.

MICK: Yeah nice one sarge.

TOBY: Don't look at me, I'm coming with you.

LEE: Oh good, sarge.

MICK: What about your feet sarge.

TOBY: Just have to manage, won't I.

MICK: But will you be all right up there sarge.

TOBY: I appreciate your concern, Pike.

LEE: You're going to need your feet up there sarge.

MICK: You need to take care of yourself sarge.

TOBY: Think I'll be a burden Pike. Will I be a burden to you.

LEE: It'll be great sarge. It'll be great to have you there.

SANDRA enters from somewhere inside the house.

SANDRA: Is he still here?

TOBY: Just till we find somewhere else for him, love.

SANDRA: Why don't you put him in the sheepshed with the others.

TOBY: He got in a fight, see.

SANDRA: How do you mean, he got in a fight. I thought that was what you was here for.

MICK: (*To SANDRA.*) It's ridiculous isn't it. See what it is, we have to look at these things as Englishmen. An Englishman should not fear to be ridiculous. Because an Englishman knows that life is ridiculous. An Englishman should expect to be ridiculous and proud of it.

SANDRA: I want to go home.

MICK: Why. Where are you from?

SANDRA: We're from Brixton.

MICK: You're not from here then.

SANDRA: No.

MICK: So did you and your husband have any knowledge of sheep before you came here?

SANDRA: You know Brixton? You know what it's like in Brixton? War, that's what it is. Cars burning in the streets, riot police, people running round covered in blood. Peter and I decided to start again. Somewhere really far away from Brixton. Somewhere really unspoiled. We chose here.

MICK: Yes you need a sense of humour.

SANDRA: We chose here. Ocean, wildflowers, grass, rocks and sheep. No more guns. No more wogs. No more men in uniform running through my back garden. No more helicopters outside my kitchen window.

MICK: Yes you certainly come to the right place.

SANDRA: I keep asking myself, is it us. Is it me. Is it my fault.

ADAM enters, with mugs.

SANDRA: Are you going to wash those.

ADAM: Sarge.

SANDRA: I felt really free coming to live out here. Because nature doesn't press on you the way people do. Now I look round and I've got helicopters breeding out of my suitcases, and soldiers swarming out of my clothes, I feel as if I've brought the plague with me.

ADAM: Can I speak to you sarge.

SANDRA: We'll never be rid of it now. There'll always be soldiers now. Tarmac everywhere, roads, barracks, wire fences and army land, that's what it will be. They'll tread everything flat and piss all over it.

MICK: That's gratitude.

SANDRA: Up till now, these islands used to sparkle.

ADAM: Where's your husband.

SANDRA: Out mending fences you knocked over.

MICK: That's gratitude.

SANDRA: If you don't like what I'm saying, you can piss off.

ADAM: All right Finch? (*He summons FINCH over to him and they prepare to remove LARRY.*)

TOBY: (*To ADAM.*) What you doing.

ADAM: Moving him out sarge.

TOBY: Did you ask my permission to move him out.

ADAM: Oh for fuck's sake.

TOBY: Did you ask my permission.

ADAM: For fuck's sake.

SANDRA: Call yourselves civilized. You filthy animals. Have you ever been to the mainland? They could buy and sell the UK. Think you're so superior. You should spend a day in the capital, it's fantastic, I'm telling you, compared with London, fantastic, and they've got a Gucci. And a Harrods. Beautiful buildings, big avenues, pavement cafes... (*To ADAM.*) Have you ever been there?

ADAM: No and I'm not fucking going there.

SANDRA: Yes well that's typical that is.

ADAM: Yes I hope so.

LEE: They think we're cannibals, they keep on talking about little black men from the jungle.

MICK: That's the gurkhas.

LEE: No the gurkhas are vegetarians, they eat pickles and that.

MICK: That's gherkins Lee.

LEE: They think we're going to cut their heads off.

MICK: Well I know a guy from Coulsdon that's brought a samurai sword along.

LEE: There's guys that have brought automatics, there's combat knives, there's all sorts.

SANDRA: My son's at school over there.

ADAM: Is he.

SANDRA: I go over twice a year.

ADAM: Yes and what about the poor people.

SANDRA: Eh.

ADAM: All this Gucci and Harrods, but what about the poor people.

SANDRA: You can talk, but you haven't seen them.

ADAM: Treat them like filth.

SANDRA: They live like filth. Little girls of ten having children by their brothers.

ADAM: Shoot anyone that complains.

SANDRA: Best thing to do with them.

ADAM: You're a nice woman.

SANDRA: Well it is. People that won't stand on their own feet, people that won't go out and get a life for themselves.

ADAM: There isn't enough lives to go round though, is there.

SANDRA: Is that my fault? Is that my problem?

ADAM: Why don't you go and live there if you like it so much, you'd save us a fuck of a lot of trouble.

SANDRA: Yes I could live there.

ADAM: Stupid cow.

MICK: I'd live anywhere compared with here.

SANDRA: What's wrong with here then?

MICK: Does this place have a tree?

SANDRA: We don't have the cheap attractions of some places.

ADAM: Sarge.

TOBY: Yes wait, you can wait.

MICK: You mean like vegetation. Habitation. Life.

SANDRA: This place is seen to best advantage when there isn't anybody here.

ADAM: I can understand the logic of that yes.

SANDRA: (*Pointedly ignoring ADAM.*) The spring here is beautiful. It's beautiful with the sun shining, and the wind blowing the grass all up the hillsides and the quiet in the valleys. The little flowers are amazing.

ADAM: Are they. The little flowers.

SANDRA: Sea pinks along the headlands, daisies, there's actually a daisy that smells like chocolate, they call it the vanilla daisy.

ADAM: Well that's intelligent.

TOBY: Who's invaded you, Sandra, us or them?

SANDRA: That's a good question, that is.

TOBY: No say what you think, by all means say what you
    think, Sandra. That's the point, actually. That's the
    point of why we're here. What you say disturbs me,
    Sandra. But I listen politely while you say it. Which is
    only right and proper I should. Because we're here to
    protect your freedom of speech. Even if what you say is
    rubbish. I might think what you say is rubbish but my
    job is to protect you. Including from myself. That's the
    difference, Sandra. That is what distinguishes us. The
    British military undertakes not only to control its
    enemies but also itself. Now, if we weren't here, and
    also they weren't here, you could say what you like. But
    they are here. And you cannot say what you like to
    them because they will not let you, and they will kill
    you. So it's a good thing you've got us here as well.
    Because we can ensure not only that you're safe from
    them but also that you're safe from us. This is why I'm
    proud to serve my country. It's a free country. It's a
    better country...

SANDRA: (*Silently stares at TOBY then returns her attention
    to MICK and LEE.*) The air in this place is normally so
    clean, you notice the change when you get within a mile
    of town, you start smelling the petrol, that's how clean
    the air is normally. Normally you could go round the
    beaches and see elephant seals. The animals never
    learned the fear of man. God they must be thick. I have
    to get the dinner.

LEE: We've eaten thanks.

SANDRA: Not for you.

MICK: We ate our dinner three hours ago.

SANDRA: You ate your dinner at ten o'clock in the morning.

MICK: Yes, we're still on the time they've got back home. To avoid confusion.

SANDRA: To avoid confusion. What time does the other side think it is?

TOBY: (*To SANDRA.*) They have the same time as you do, Sandra.

SANDRA: You mean they have the actual time which sane people have.

TOBY: Yes, except in the town which we're informed is two hours later conforming to the time on the mainland.

SANDRA: Oh I see.

TOBY: Being three hours ahead may seem strange to you, but it gives us the advantage of surprise.

SANDRA: Surprised! I bet they're surprised! I should think they were fucking amazed.

TOBY: No seriously Sandra, Zulu Time is a tactical weapon.

SANDRA: Zulu Time. Is that what you call it! Zulu Time. And you mean to say, you've got my life in your hands.

TOBY: I'm glad you find it so amusing, Sandra.

LEE: British isn't it.

MICK: British and proud of it.

LEE: Even if it's stupid we're proud if it's British.

MICK: Especially if it's stupid we're proud if it's British.

LEE: Anyone can be proud of things that are clever.

MICK: That's not loyalty, being proud of things that are clever. Loyalty only comes into it when you're proud of things that are utterly utterly stupid.

ADAM: Sarge. Can I speak to you.

LARRY: Fuck you.

SANDRA: He speaks English.

TOBY: (*To LARRY.*) No that won't do, I'm not having that, you behave yourself.

LARRY: Fuck you.

SANDRA: (*To LARRY.*) Excuse me where are you from?

LARRY: (*To SANDRA.*) These fucking assholes.

SANDRA: Excuse me are you American?

LARRY: I told them. I told them.

LEE: Is he American?

LARRY: I was like, glad to know you, I'm American. Then they start beating the crap out of me.

LEE: (*To LARRY.*) You cunt.

LARRY: What's the matter with them?

LEE: Where's your loyalty?

LARRY: Where's yours? We speak the same language here.

LEE: You fucking traitor!

LARRY: Neutral. I'm a neutral. (*Yawns.*)

LEE: Don't yawn at me, you cunt.

LARRY: (*Yawns.*)

LEE: You see that. You see him yawn. You want to die, you cunt, is that it. You want to die. You yawn at me once more you'll fucking die.

LARRY: (*Yawns.*)

LEE: (*LEE yawns.*) Fuck. (*Looks around at the others then back at LARRY.*) You'll pay for this.

LARRY: (*Yawns.*)

LEE: (*Yawns.*) Oh fuck! Fucking Yank taking the piss. (*Yawns.*) I'm going to kill you now.

TOBY: Finch. He's frightened, Finch.

MICK: Yes Lee, you frightened him.

LEE: I'll frighten him. I'll frighten him.

TOBY: He's yawning because he's frightened. Sleep is fear.

ADAM: You'd know, you cunt.

TOBY: Sleep is a strategy for putting an end to conflict.

LEE: Put an end to conflict. Him. (*To LARRY.*) We'll put an end to conflict when we're fucking ready. Fucking nerve. Fucking Yank.

SANDRA: What's he doing here, if he's American?

TOBY: (*To SANDRA.*) He's got nothing to complain of, Sandra, there's plenty in worse shape than him.

ADAM: (*To SANDRA.*) We're trying to get this man home. We're trying to get hold of some transport to take him back home. If he'd behave himself, our job would be that much easier.

SANDRA: What's he doing in that uniform?

ADAM: That's it, Sandra, he's nothing but trouble, what does he want. The Hilton.

LARRY: I'm not going anywhere with him.

ADAM: What does he want. Club Class.

LARRY: (*To SANDRA.*) I'm not going anywhere with him.

SANDRA: Is he a mercenary?

ADAM: We're taking him out of here now.

SANDRA: (*To LARRY.*) You scum.

ADAM: He shouldn't have been in here in the first place.

TOBY: No he shouldn't, corporal.

SANDRA: (*To TOBY.*) Why didn't you find somewhere!

TOBY: Now wait a minute Sandra, I never said they could put him in here, it wasn't me said put him in here.

SANDRA: That scum, and you knew this, and you let them bring him in here, into my home, into my kitchen...

TOBY: You're like my wife, Sandra, she's like you.

SANDRA: What the fuck are you talking about?

TOBY: She wants the place just the way she wants it.

SANDRA: Eh.

MICK: He has to take his shoes off before she'll let him through the door. Socks is all she lets him wear.

LEE: She's got beautiful furniture.

MICK: She's got a beautiful Spanish style coffee table.

SANDRA: Get him out.

ADAM: (*He makes to take LARRY out.*) Come on.

LARRY: No.

TOBY: What's so amusing Pike. What's so amusing about a Spanish style coffee table? Can't you take anything seriously?

SANDRA: (*To TOBY.*) What are you talking about, you arsehole!

TOBY: I've gone out of my way to look after you Sandra. Which is part of my job to do, to help you remain innocent and (*He sees the hand on the floor, tries to kick it out of sight.*) safe...

MICK: What's the matter sarge?

LEE: What's the matter sarge are you all right?

TOBY: (*He kicks the hand again.*) What is this.

SANDRA: My God.

Silence.

LEE: Where's that dog.

TOBY: Sandra don't be alarmed.

SANDRA: Oh yes it's funny is it. Waiting for me to set eyes on that. Good joke, is it.

TOBY: Don't be alarmed, Sandra, don't be alarmed...

SANDRA: (*To the others, ignoring TOBY.*) Think it's rubbish here don't you. Think we're rubbish. How you can make out you want to fight for us.. You want to fight because you want to fight and that's all. And if we're rubbish. What are you. You're dossers. If you weren't doing this. You'd all be on the social. If it wasn't for all this. Where would you be. Living in some flat on some estate, and your biggest thrill of the day would be cutting your toenails with the breadknife. Dregs of society, you are. Get yourselves killed, best thing for everyone.

MICK: That's nice, that is. That's nice.

SANDRA: You're fortunate the weather's been so mild.

ADAM: Fifteen days of freezing rain, you call that mild.

SANDRA: We'll be getting the blizzards. You'll be fucked then. There'll be snow blowing by the ton. You'll have no transport. Nothing will fly. Your ships will fuck off home without you and leave you to perish. Mind where you are when it starts, because that's where you'll stay. (*She gets a brush and pan and sweeps up the hand, then throws hand, dustpan and brush into the bin.*)

ADAM: Don't get rid of that, I was intending to dry that out, love, and use it for an ashtray.

SANDRA: It's such a crying shame. That the opposite sex. Had to be men.

TOBY: He'll apologize, love, the corporal will apologize.

SANDRA: I'm not the one leaving this room. You're the ones leaving this room.

TOBY: The corporal will apologize. You're going to have to straighten out your thinking, for your own sake corporal, for your own sake, because you're damaging yourself with this arrogance, it's yourself whom you're damaging, far more than others. You may never even see the damage you've done to yourself, it's going to eat away at your career and hollow you out in ways you never even see. Till you're nothing but a shell. Nothing but bluster and impudence. I give orders to you because that is my right, which I've earned by my own achievements, known, measured, attested and rewarded by those who have the power and responsibility of deciding these matters. A man may dream of giving orders without having been awarded the necessary rank, but if his dreams start taking the place of reality then that man's dream becomes a danger to everyone's real and serious business. That man becomes a liability.

ADAM: A liability. Yes. Yes he does.

TOBY: You're embarked on a dangerous course corporal.

ADAM: I thought it was a fucking picnic sarge.

TOBY: If that's aimed at me, corporal.

ADAM: You fucking disaster! Years you've been trained and held in readiness. Just in order that now, at the crucial moment, you'd be in a position to demonstrate your total incompetence!

TOBY: If that's aimed at me.

ADAM: This is the climax to years of preparation. Where you stand revealed as a complete and utter nothing. A vapour trail swelling into nothingness.

SANDRA: I'm not the one leaving this room.

ADAM: Fuck off love. Go on. Fuck off.

SANDRA leaves.

TOBY: I would have been there last night. I would have been there. This time, when you go, I'm going up there.

ADAM: I don't advise it.

TOBY: Why.

ADAM: It's dangerous.

TOBY: Oh yes.

ADAM: I mean for you. You cunt. If you're up there with me. It's dangerous for you. Finch take this man outside.

LEE: It's freezing.

ADAM: Take him outside.

LARRY: (*To TOBY.*) No.

TOBY: You've made enough trouble, shut your face.

FINCH and LARRY off.

TOBY: You better clean the floor, Pike.

ADAM: Sarge there's something I have to discuss.

TOBY: Don't use the dish cloth Pike.

MICK: Sorry.

TOBY: Did you never learn how to clean things Pike? Don't people clean things in Liverpool? Just cry on them do they, just cry on them cause they're such sorry Liverpool cunts.

ADAM: I've been on the radio sarge.

TOBY: Desert Island Discs was it. Again Pike. Clean it again.

MICK: It's clean sarge.

TOBY: Yes but you've touched it haven't you. Clean it again. After that, you can wash those mugs.

ADAM: Pike, piss off.

TOBY: He's not going anywhere, not till those mugs are washed, Sandra's not doing them, no reason why she should do them is there.

ADAM: Piss off, Pike.

MICK: (*To TOBY.*) Sarge?

TOBY: Glad enough to accept a brew, aren't you Pike, we're all of us glad enough to accept a brew, well sooner or later the time comes along you have to pay for it.

ADAM: Pike.

MICK off.

TOBY: What rank are you lance corporal. What rank do you take yourself for. Seemingly you're not a lance corporal, lance corporal, you're not merely some piss-ignorant cunt of a mere lance corporal, it's almost as if you seem to be under the illusion, lance corporal, that you're my superior officer whereas in fact, lance corporal, the reverse is the case.

ADAM: Sarge.

TOBY: I should make you wash those.

ADAM: I've been on the radio.

TOBY: I should make you wash those. Do the fucking things myself. (*He starts washing mugs.*)

ADAM: Will you listen!

TOBY: Where's the tea towel.

ADAM: He says. We're to shoot the American.

TOBY: (*Drops a mug.*) Eh.

ADAM: Eh.

TOBY: Bollocks.

ADAM: Eh.

TOBY: What does he mean, shoot him.

ADAM: Well sarge, how many ways can you think of to interpret that.

TOBY: What for.

ADAM: (*Patiently.*) It's an order sarge.

TOBY: Whose order. That little twat.

ADAM: Yes sarge.

TOBY: That little tosser.

ADAM: Your superior officer, sarge.

TOBY: I don't have to stand for this.

ADAM: Really sarge. Really.

TOBY: No he can't mean this. You can't have heard him right.

ADAM: I what.

TOBY: You can't have heard him right.

ADAM: Do you think I'm deaf.

TOBY: I never said you're deaf.

ADAM: If you think I'm deaf, why don't you say so.

TOBY: I never said you're deaf, only I thought you said to me the batteries...

ADAM: There's nothing wrong with the batteries.

TOBY: Nevertheless you did say to me the batteries...

ADAM: There's absolutely fuck-all wrong with the batteries. Were you put on earth to drive me mad?

TOBY: I just want to make sure I've got this straight.

ADAM: You were. You were put on this earth to drive me mad. Because if they can't get you with the big stuff, they get you with the little stuff, the little, weak, incredibly irritating stuff...

TOBY: I'm only suggesting the radio might...

ADAM: All right, you talk to him.

TOBY: No no, I wasn't suggesting...

ADAM: You don't trust what I say, you talk to him.

TOBY: I never said I don't trust what you say.

ADAM: Take the fucking radio. Talk to him. Take the fucking radio.

TOBY: I don't need the radio.

ADAM: Take it you cunt!

TOBY: No no I don't want the radio. I don't want the radio.

ADAM: Why can't you trust what I say. What is the matter with you. Why did you have to be my sergeant.

TOBY: Where's the dustpan.

ADAM: Why did they have to bring you here.

TOBY: Where's the dustpan. (*Remembers where it is.*) Oh yes.

ADAM: Why couldn't they have left you quietly somewhere in the barracks to die.

TOBY: Just like that. Shoot him, just like that.

ADAM: Can you think of some other way of shooting him, sarge.

TOBY: He gave himself up. He's a prisoner.

ADAM: So he is.

TOBY: Why.

ADAM: Who knows.

TOBY: Trouble with the Americans. They'll be panicking over the thought of trouble with the Americans. I'm being asked to murder a man in case of trouble with the Americans. And he's an American. Oh yes, it makes absolute sense.

ADAM: Yes sarge. As soon as possible sarge.

TOBY: I'm trying to think.

ADAM: Stop thinking, sarge, and concentrate.

TOBY: I can't.

ADAM: No sarge.

TOBY: I can't think, because I can't find where anything is, corporal. Everything is in a different place. The air. I used to think it was safe. Now it's got bullets in it. A clear sky. I used to think a clear sky was empty. Now I see a plane come out of it with a bomb. Grass. I used to think it's for walking on. Now each time anyone puts their foot down I think he's treading on a mine.

ADAM: I don't need this. I'm so fucking tired. I don't need this.

TOBY: I haven't debriefed him. He may have information.

ADAM: I'm tired of information.

TOBY: Well it's all very well to talk about these things but to actually pick up a gun and do it, to pick up a gun and do it now, well I'd like to see anyone that would enjoy the idea.

ADAM: Least of all you sarge.

TOBY: All right. If that's the way you see it. If that's the way you want it. You want the responsibility, you take it. That's what you're saying to me. You're saying to me, you think I'm not fit. So what you come running to me for. You do whatever seems best to you. Do what you think best.

ADAM: I'll shoot him then, shall I sarge.

TOBY: Nothing to do with me.

ADAM: I'll shoot him.

TOBY: Don't know what I'm worrying about. More trouble than he's worth. We've lads of our own to worry about.

ADAM: That's right.

TOBY: He doesn't deserve it.

ADAM: That's right sarge.

TOBY: World's upside down in any case, what difference does it make.

ADAM: That's right sarge, you forget about it sarge.

TOBY: You think I wouldn't do it.

ADAM: No sarge, no, I don't think anything sarge.

TOBY: Do it if I have to.

ADAM: I'm not saying you wouldn't sarge.

TOBY: I could, you know.

ADAM: Do you want to do it, sarge?

TOBY: Oh no not me, too much of a fucking coward, aren't I, no no, you're the one that wants to do it, you fucking do it.

ADAM: Suit yourself.

TOBY: No point my doing it, is there, it wouldn't change anything.

ADAM: No sarge.

TOBY: I'd still be a fucking coward, wouldn't I.

ADAM: Yes sarge.

TOBY: You'd still be wanting to put a bullet in me. I don't know. It might come as a relief.

ADAM: To all of us, sarge.

TOBY: Yes I do see that. I do see that.

ADAM: Not your fault sarge. Made that way. Some people are made that way.

TOBY: They shouldn't be. Should they.

ADAM: We can't choose how we're made.

TOBY: I expect you mean well by that. Thank you.

ADAM: Better get on, sarge. Things to do.

TOBY: I'm going to come out of this.

ADAM: Better get on.

TOBY: No listen to me. I'm going to come out of this now. I've hit the bottom of this, and now I'm coming up out of it. I'm not going to let you do this thing.

ADAM: Eh.

TOBY: You don't understand. We shouldn't be doing this thing.

ADAM: Oh fucking hell.

TOBY: It's not right, corporal.

ADAM: Oh fuck me.

TOBY: You think I'm a coward. I'm not such a coward that I'm going to let you do this. The task of the military.

ADAM: Eh.

TOBY: The task of the military is to make things reliable, even things which are not reliable.

ADAM: Eh.

TOBY: That order's against the law.

ADAM: An order is the law, sarge.

TOBY: No, orders change but the law remains reliable.

ADAM: Don't start please sarge.

TOBY: He's not a traitor.

ADAM: Don't fucking start.

TOBY: He's not a traitor. He's a neutral we thought was on our side.

ADAM: Well put, sarge.

TOBY: Supposing it gets out that we shot him.

ADAM: It's not as if I like it sarge.

TOBY: We'll be the ones take the blame.

ADAM: But that's what we've come here for, to do things we don't like. I say to myself, if I don't like it, that proves it must be right, because that's what we've come here for.

TOBY: There are people up there looking down on all of this.

ADAM: No there aren't, sarge.

TOBY: Just because we're tiny it doesn't mean we're invisible. People up there can see anything they want, they're not stupid the people up there.

ADAM: Up where, sarge. Up in the sky are they sarge.

TOBY: They can see you, and me, and all the other thousands that are here. And if once they focus on you, you won't be tiny, you'll be magnified thousands of times in those eyes of theirs, and everything you've done will be seen. How will you feel about that. When that speck of dirt is caught and magnified thousands of times in those great big eyes, and nothing in your life is ever the same again.

ADAM: I don't really think anyone up there is bothered sarge.

TOBY: Yes they are.

ADAM: You know that, do you sarge.

TOBY: Well at the very least they're people, the people up there. I've met them, some of them. They talk like people, behave like people, I'm a person, it bothers me, are they immune? no, how could they be, if I'm a person, they must be more so, otherwise why would they be up there. They wouldn't be up there if they was less, they have to be more, don't they. Mrs Thatcher herself is a mother.

ADAM: I tell you who will be bothered sarge. He'll be bothered.

TOBY: That little twat.

ADAM: If we don't carry out this order, he'll be bothered. Our lives won't be worth living. Will they sarge.

TOBY: What are we, murderers. I'm not a lackey. I'm a free man who's freely chosen to fight in defence of the laws of my country. I'm not the hired help. That little twat. Thinks that's all we're fit for. Get back to him corporal. Ask him for confirmation.

ADAM: Confirmation?

TOBY: Yes.

ADAM: Confirmation.

TOBY: Yes.

ADAM: (*His patience is absolutely exhausted.*) Oh yes of course. Confirmation.

TOBY: Tell him I want it confirmed from higher up.

ADAM: Yes but sarge, he will get it confirmed from higher up.

TOBY: He won't.

ADAM: They're mounting an attack. They're busy, sarge.

TOBY: That doesn't mean they'll confirm whatever he says.

ADAM: It's hardly the time to question an order sarge.

TOBY: They have to be better than that. Otherwise, what am I doing here.

ADAM: I don't know sarge, I really don't know.

TOBY: They operate in the full light of day up there. Not like us in the dark. It's part of their job to ensure that we are in the right. That's their part of the bargain. It's for them to ensure that we are in the right, so that we can go into action feeling confident. Their job is to make it right, then we can feel confident and secure about making it happen.

ADAM: Oh good, sarge.

TOBY: You'll get back to him, corporal.

ADAM: If I get back to him, and they confirm it, will you be happy.

TOBY: Yes but they won't. They won't. They wouldn't. (*ADAM off.*) Because I don't see the point of us fighting the other side if we're no better than they are. Unless we're simply fighting to win, and for no other reason. I wouldn't mind fighting to win, as such. But dying to win. Me dying. Simply in order for them up there to win. And them up there being no better than the other lot. I'd have to think about that.

...Once I was sure that she and the brass were all safely inside, I had to step out the lift, turn round and salute while the doors were closing. Then, as she began to ascend, I had to run like buggery up three flights of stairs so as to be standing there outside the lift at attention, not out of breath, ready to salute her as the doors opened up again...

SECOND SECTION

Later the same day. SANDRA and ADAM in her son's bedroom.

SANDRA: We should never have sent him to that school. How can he hold his head up in that school with all of this going on? What must they be doing to him. I never wanted to send him to that school. It was Peter who said we're sending him to that school. There's never any discussion, you know what I mean.

ADAM: No discussion. How does he manage that, then.

SANDRA: Peter always goes to bed at eight o'clock. Every night. He's up again at five o'clock. Hot breakfast every morning. He chews everything thirty times. He read it in a book.

ADAM: So where's this school then.

SANDRA: And here's my son's room just waiting here. For all the good this room's doing him, it might as well not exist. And by the time he comes home, perhaps it won't exist. Perhaps this house won't even be left standing. So I hope Peter's satisfied.

ADAM: He speaks Spanish, your son, does he.

SANDRA: More than you do.

ADAM: I speak English. I prefer it.

SANDRA: Then you can just wallow in your ignorance, can't you.

ADAM: They're the ignorant ones. What's he going to learn from them, except their ignorance.

SANDRA: This is the best room to see from. Peter and I were in here last night watching, it was better than Guy Fawkes.

ADAM: That's where I was, up there.

SANDRA: What's all the white bits on the grass up there.

ADAM: Field dressings.

SANDRA: Eh.

ADAM: They press them on wounds to control the bleeding.

SANDRA: Dreadful.

ADAM: Carrying men around with drips in their arms, don't know if you're in a battle or a hospital.

SANDRA: It turns my stomach. (*They kiss.*)

ADAM: You're a strange one. (*He turns to go.*)

SANDRA: Don't go, I'm frightened, you make me feel safe.

ADAM: I what.

ADAM off. After a moment, TOBY comes in.

TOBY: The corporal's not in here.

SANDRA: No.

TOBY: Your one area of sanity.

SANDRA: Oh definitely.

TOBY: I'd like to apologise, Sandra, for the events in your kitchen.

SANDRA: Nothing you could do, was there.

TOBY: I'm still responsible Sandra. I'm still responsible. I'm sorry you had to see such a thing. See it once, it's with you forever.

SANDRA: Yes thanks for reminding me, thank you very much.

TOBY: And you've got to cook in there.

SANDRA: Yes, fish fingers will take on a whole new meaning.

TOBY: My wife's allergic, you know.

SANDRA: Oh. What's she allergic to. Personally, I'm allergic to bits of dead people in my kitchen.

TOBY: Sensitive yes. She's almost completed a wine tasting course. Seventeen kinds of champagne. And her palate was able to differentiate between them all. She tasted the lot. Seventeen glasses. She spits it out of course. Fastidious you see. A sergeant's wife has to set an example. Her garden has to be weeded. Her doorstep has to be scrubbed. My wife's doorstep is as clean as most women's pillows. Look Sandra. I've apologized.

SANDRA: Yes.

TOBY: You could try to be a bit more understanding, Sandra.

SANDRA: What's that mean.

TOBY: Not everyone's in your bad books.

SANDRA: What are you talking about?

TOBY: I saw the two of you chatting on the stairs. That savage. If you can stomach that, Sandra, well then.

SANDRA: What.

TOBY: Well then.

SANDRA: What.

TOBY: So what would be the prospects for me.

SANDRA: You're all the same, you're all the fucking same.

TOBY: The question is bound to arise, Sandra, if him, then why not...

SANDRA: You poor broken-down watery-eyed little sod.

TOBY: I don't think that's quite fair Sandra, but be that as it may, Sandra, I need a little bit of light, that's all, a bit of light shining on me from your face, that's all, a bit of warmth to save me... No, I'm sorry. I'm sorry. I know it hasn't been easy for you... I'm sorry about your toilet Sandra. I advised it should be placed out of bounds. Others disagreed with me. I'm sorry about your goose. It may come back. It may just have gone for a walk. I'm sorry about the trenches in your lawn. Anyway you might be glad of one yourself if our presence draws an air raid to this place.

SANDRA: Oh thanks very much. Yes thank you.

TOBY: I'm sorry Sandra.

SANDRA: How much do they pay you.

TOBY: That mercenary probably makes ten times what I do. But what are they, they're just cowboys, ghouls, they're mad, they've got to be fighting, blow their legs off they'd try and sign up in a wheelchair. They're doing it for kicks you see, selfish, running wild, you can't tell them anything, mercenaries is all they're fit for. They're not good men Sandra. They hold nothing sacred. Not even violence. But no. I'm lucky enough to be serving in a volunteer force which is both moral and necessary, defending democracy, freedom and the law.

SANDRA: Don't you love your country then.

TOBY: Eh.

SANDRA: Do you only love your country because it's a democracy? What if it wasn't a democracy? Wouldn't you love it then?

TOBY: I'd have to think about that, Sandra.

SANDRA: You don't love it then, do you. If you have to stop and think, it means you don't love it.

TOBY: No no wait a minute Sandra, there has to be an element of reason.

SANDRA: That's what I say. You don't love it.

TOBY: No that's not patriotism. That's hysteria.

SANDRA: I love my son. Whatever he does. I love him now and always. Whatever he does. Are you calling me hysterical?

TOBY: No Sandra, of course not, no, all things considered, but put it this way Sandra I might love my country whatever it does, but that's not to say I'd fight for my country whatever it does.

SANDRA: Oh.

TOBY: What does that mean. Oh. What does that mean.

LEE and ADAM enter, with LARRY.

TOBY: What's this. (*No response.*) What you bring him up here for.

ADAM: It's all right sarge, don't worry yourself.

TOBY: I never said you could bring him up here.

ADAM: No sarge.

TOBY: Did I say you could bring him up here.

ADAM: It's all right sarge.

TOBY: Take him downstairs.

ADAM: He's better off up here sarge.

TOBY: Take him down.

ADAM: He's out of the way up here.

TOBY: I promised Sandra, nobody in this room.

ADAM: You promised Sandra.

TOBY: Yes.

ADAM: Keeping on the right side of Sandra, were you.

TOBY: Have you got anything against that, corporal?

ADAM: Looking after Sandra's interests.

TOBY: Eh.

ADAM: She can see through you. She doesn't want any favours from you sarge. Do you Sandra.

SANDRA: I said to Adam he can put him in this room.

TOBY: You said to Adam .

SANDRA: I said he can put him in this room. Is that all right with you?

TOBY: This is the thanks I get.

ADAM: What thanks were you expecting sarge.

TOBY: Eh. What do you mean. How dare you.

ADAM: I said to Sandra, just till we know what his transport's going to be. Just till we know when he's able to go back home.

TOBY: Have you –

ADAM: No sarge.

TOBY: Why not, corporal. Why haven't you –

ADAM: I can't get through to him sarge.

TOBY: Try again.

ADAM: Yes sarge.

TOBY off. LARRY goes and lies on the floor in a corner, falls asleep.

SANDRA: (*Referring to TOBY.*) What you give him such a hard time for.

LEE: He's a sergeant, isn't he.

SANDRA: The state of him though. I think it's all too much for him.

ADAM: Yes he's exhausted by his efforts to stay out of combat.

SANDRA: What you so mean to him for.

LEE: Sergeants are so boring, everyone hates them. Everyone hates them cause everyone wants to be mad. And sergeants want to be sane. They want to be sane so badly. They wind up being madder than all the rest of us put together.

SANDRA: (*To ADAM.*) Are you coming out of here?

LEE: No, this is it, they have an impossible task, because they have to train us.

ADAM: He's got a point there.

LEE: They have to train us to be hard, see, which means they have to be hard on us. There was one used to get me up five o'clock every morning my first three weeks. Out running before the sun came up, all round the barracks with ice all over the roads and they'd be shouting at us how we were the worst they'd ever had, so weak, no puff, they were all day telling me how thick I was and I'd never make it, it's just, I like to stop and think but you're never supposed to, so they're all the time making out I'm a halfwit because I have thoughts.

ADAM: Yes but Finch, they're halfwitted thoughts.

LEE: I don't see how you make that out.

ADAM: (*To SANDRA.*) Recruiting officers give you a little intelligence test, nothing very taxing you understand, nothing very difficult. They score them, one two three four five. Fours and fives they can't be doing with.

They're too stupid even for the military. But they chuck out the ones as well. They don't want the ones, cause the ones might ask questions. Twos and threes are their favourites, twos and threes. Smart enough to fight. Dumb enough not to ask why.

LEE: (*Continuing his talk to SANDRA.*) They break you right down, they make sure you know exactly how bad life can be when they don't respect you, nothing you do seems to please them and they make you feel like a boil on the face of the earth. Then one day you do something right and someone gives you a good word suggesting they don't hate you quite as much as before. So then the joy of living starts up again, it's like you're born again and they've become your parents, a few weeks down the line and by then you're well in. You're not allowed home the first six weeks. They know what they're doing see. By that time they've become your family, you've won the acceptance and you're really happy they let you belong. Only that's why it comes as a bit of a shock when they let you go off and get killed, because families aren't supposed to be like that.

ADAM: You're just a number, Finch, to be crunched in that big black mouth.

LEE: But this is the sergeant's problem. Because the reason he takes the trouble to be hard on you is that he cares. The more he cares, the more he treats you like a bastard. The more he treats you like a bastard, the more he cares. I don't think it's good for them. They get really strange, some of them. They get really nice to you. It's horrible.

SANDRA: (*To ADAM.*) Are you going to stay in here?

ADAM: No.

SANDRA: I'm down the hall.

SANDRA off.

LEE: She's down the hall.

ADAM: She is.

LEE: Are you going down the hall?

ADAM: Might do. I don't want her coming back in.

LEE: No, that's right, no.

ADAM: Shut your face Lee.

LEE: Amazing though.

ADAM: What.

LEE: It's everywhere.

ADAM: Are you clear in your mind about what you're going to do?

LEE: Tell you the truth, I'm not really in the mood you know. It's our day off, you know.

MICK enters.

You have to keep on, don't you, it's like the dog in the cartoon, he runs over a cliff and just keeps on running, he can run along in thin air just as long as he doesn't look down. Once he looks down, he falls.

ADAM off.

MICK: The way I look at it. An order which is so obviously questionable has to be, by definition, an order that was made with very good reason. It's not as if they like making questionable orders. So obviously if he finds he has to make an order like that, such an obviously questionable order, the last thing he wants is for anyone to question it.

LEE: Sooner we get this over with.

MICK: The problem with something like this. A questionable order like this. We assume it results out of careful deliberation. We assume there are special circumstances.

LEE: I'm so tired.

MICK: We assume that all the careful deliberation which people have been doing for years has finally resulted in someone having the right to make this questionable order in special circumstances.

LEE: So tired.

MICK: Of course all the time it might just have come from some twat.

LEE starts spreading a poncho on the floor.

I don't like this in the house.

LEE: No.

MICK: Why am I here. (*Pause.*) Do you want a drink?

LEE: Yeah.

MICK leaves. LARRY lies still for a while, then, half asleep, gets up and starts climbing into the bed.

LEE: Get off that.

LARRY: No.

LEE: Here's where you should lie, get over here.

LARRY: Clean cotton. So smooth. I can't feel it.

LEE: You can't get in there. You have to kip here.

LARRY: It's so little.

LEE: You won't fit in there.

LARRY: Yes I will.

LEE: I'm warning you.

LARRY: I'm getting in here and I'm staying in here.

LEE: You're disgusting. You're filthy.

LARRY: This your room?

LEE: Doesn't have to be mine for me to know what's right.

LARRY: Yes it does.

LEE: Yes but you should know what's right as well. You should know what's right as well.

LARRY: I don't.

LEE: (*Threatening LARRY with a gun.*) Get off.

LARRY: Like you said. You know what's right. I have to sleep.

LEE: Get off.

LARRY: I'm ready to die so long as I die right here. (*Closes his eyes.*)

LEE: (*Goes over and shakes him.*) Come on wake up.

LARRY: (*Half asleep.*) Haven't slept in thirty-six hours.

LEE: (*Yelling in his ear.*) Neither have I! (*Slaps LARRY's face.*) Right. Keep them open. Selfish cunt. I can't sleep. Can I! I can't sleep and it's on account of you! I'm supposed to be resting! I'm going to die because of you! I won't see the danger when it's coming. My eyes will be too tired to move. I'll be dead, and it will be your fault!

LARRY: Quiet.

LEE: (*He grabs a toy drum and bashes it.*) Sleepy? (*Bashes the drum again.*) Night night! (*Bashes the drum again.*)

TOBY enters and watches him for a moment.

TOBY: What are you doing, Finch?

LEE: Nothing sarge.

TOBY: I could have sworn I heard a noise.

LEE: It's only pretend sarge.

TOBY: The face on you. Struck dumb. What would I find if I went in through your face. A thousand paths through the forest. Which one brings me to the centre.

LEE: I don't know sarge.

TOBY: Is there a centre, Finch?

LEE: I don't know sarge.

TOBY: Put the drum down Finch.

LEE: Yes sarge.

TOBY: Asleep is he.

LEE: Yes sarge.

TOBY: We have to treat him properly, Finch. There's no end to what he might be able to tell us, there's no end to what we might be able to learn, if only we treat him properly.

LEE: Yes sarge.

TOBY: Hardly going the right way about it, are you Finch.

LEE: No sarge.

TOBY: Who knows what's inside that head of his. There's only one way to get that information out. By the delicate mechanism of speech. By carefully encouraging those mysterious little puffs of breath. We're going to have to coax the words out of him like little kittens.

LEE: Yes sarge.

TOBY: We have to be patient.

LEE: Yes sarge.

TOBY: And not smash his brains in.

LEE: Yes sarge.

TOBY: Otherwise what will become of all the little kittens.

LEE: Yes sarge.

TOBY: He shouldn't be on that bed though.

LEE: Mick and I can get him on to the floor sarge.

TOBY: Yes but nicely Finch. Be nice. With what he could tell us, fighting could well be avoided.

LEE: Yes sarge.

TOBY: Anything wrong with that, Finch?

LEE: No sarge.

TOBY: I never heard there was anything wrong with fighting being avoided, Finch.

LEE: No of course not sarge.

TOBY: It troubles me what you might be thinking.

LEE: Don't trouble yourself sarge.

TOBY: I do trouble myself. Finch. I'm walking around thinking nothing is solid. As if the ground was going to melt away from under my feet and I'd look down and see daylight through the hole. Whatever I touch, it starts to melt, as soon as my fingers touch there are hollows forming. Everything I pass through is falling into wreckage, and I can only manage to escape by moving forward. My mum and dad.

LEE: Eh.

TOBY: I never used to know what was the matter, all the time at home it was like there was a cold wind blowing on me so hard, so hard, I couldn't stand upright. And then I joined up and I wasn't living at home any more and all at once I found the wind had dropped, it had simply stopped blowing and everything was quiet, what a relief. And I slowly straightened up, and I stretched. Because what I'd learned was, there are things which work. There are things which can be controlled.

LEE: Yes sarge, thank God for that sarge, you taught us that, didn't you sarge.

TOBY: I hope you won't forget what I've taught you, Finch.

LEE: No it's really useful sarge.

TOBY: Has the corporal said anything to you.

LEE: What about, sarge.

TOBY: Good, good.

MICK enters.

If you see the corporal, Finch, tell him I'm looking for him.

TOBY off.

MICK: Wake him up, we'll have to get him off there.

LEE: Just you try, that's double sleep he's got there, that's my sleep as well he's got there.

MICK: (*Speaks in LARRY's ear.*) Larry. Wake up. We have to move you. (*No response. They shrug. To LEE.*) Here. (*He produces a bottle of whisky.*)

LEE: Where'd you get it.

MICK: Swapped some loot for it. Pistol. I've still got two more.

LEE: We'll have to move him though.

MICK: Yeah. (*They go and sit on the poncho, and drink out of the bottle.*)

LEE: See this.

MICK: That's your piece of shrapnel.

LEE: This was in my chinstrap.

MICK: Yeah, Lee, you told me.

LEE: Here. It was here.

MICK: You told me.

LEE: That would have been my eye.

MICK: Yeah, you need to be careful, Lee.

LEE: I think of it in my brain.

MICK: Yes well that's where people normally think of things.

LEE: It's almost like it's been in there and come out again knowing everything about me. I feel as if it could tell me all about myself.

MICK: Well. Good luck.

LEE: Yeah.

MICK: Why am I here.

LEE: (*Unpacking things from pockets.*) You got these? The night vision glasses? Magic these. See and not be seen. When you get married Mick I'll be standing in your bedroom with these.

MICK: Do you think we ought to move him.

LEE: Ammunition. Pack of enemy fags I'm going to take home for my mum.

MICK: Done your holiday shopping then.

LEE: All right we'll move him shall we.

MICK: I haven't thought about anything back home since we got here. How many people back home have ever been tested. How many of them would be ready die for their faith. What's your faith Lee.

LEE: Being ready to die.

MICK: Is that it.

LEE: Yeah.

MICK: I'm not really ready to die.

LEE: Aren't you?

MICK: No, Lee, I'm not.

LEE: So then. What brings you here.

MICK: Why should I die for them. All they want is a chance to get on with their selfish little imaginary little lives. I'd die for my mates. Because we've earned it. As for the rest of them. Living on in their kingdom of light with their cities and their glorious pavements and their freedom parades, walking on the dust that used to be us, well they're laughing aren't they. Fuck them. I hate them. Maybe it's not even worth hanging round if I just have to be with them. Come on, we have to move him.

LEE: See these.

MICK: (*Looks at LEE's photos.*) Ooh! pig.

LEE: Pig??

MICK: (*Grunts.*)

LEE: I don't think she's a pig, I think she's nice.

MICK: What's she written on it. Hullo soldier whoever you are, friends tell me I look like Olivia Newton John so let's get physical. No I don't think so. Where'd you get these, off the pigs' notice board. I put one or two on there, I threw the rest of mine off the ship to frighten the sharks.

LEE: These didn't come off the pigs' notice board.

MICK: Yes they did, there's dart holes in them.

LEE: Let's see.

MICK: Only joking.

LEE: I thought that was out of order, throwing darts at them.

MICK: Oh disgusting yes, having to aim at them, having to look at them, oh God that took courage, oh my God.

LEE: You're no oil painting yourself Mick.

MICK: Am I not.

LEE: No you're not.

MICK: I know that.

LEE: How would you like it if someone talked that way about you.

MICK: So what you're saying is, if I don't want to be talked about like that, I shouldn't talk like that.

LEE: Yeah. That's it, yeah.

MICK: (*Indicating picture.*) So you don't think that she would talk about anyone like that.

LEE: No. I don't think she would.

MICK: It hasn't stopped me from talking about her though. It hasn't saved her from having me talk about her. Has it. Has it.

LEE: No, but.

MICK: Well there you are then. What good has she done herself. None.

LEE: That's not what I was trying to say.

MICK: None. What were you trying to say.

LEE: I don't know. Something different.

MICK: Don't try to be different, Lee. You've got enough problems trying to be the same.

LEE: See this one though. This is a nice one, this one is really nice, this one is not a slag. She sent a picture of herself with her mum and dad in their garden see, and she writes, To a brave soldier, thank you for what you are doing for our country, we are all praying for you, love, Lorraine. She has sympathy, I know she has sympathy, she's got a really gentle face, don't you think she has, and she's got true eyes, she's sending her thoughts and I can feel them reach me.

MICK: Her thoughts eh.

LEE: Yeah.

MICK: She should send her tits. Look at them.

LEE: Yeah. What I'm going to do, if I get home, I thought I'd go and introduce myself you know, say I am the soldier who received your card and I cherished it, I kept it on me in times of danger and as you can see it must have protected me.

MICK: Nice one.

LEE: If they don't let me fuck them, what does that tell us about their patriotism.

MICK: They.

LEE: I've got nineteen.

LARRY wakes up screaming.

MICK: Here. Cut that out. (*LARRY stops screaming, stares at MICK.*) Stop that. What's your game. You stop that all right. Frightened the life out of me. Are you awake? You should be ashamed of yourself. Misbehaving yourself like that. Give you a spanking I will if you do that. Don't try to make me sorry for you, carrying on like that. The only thing you make me feel is disgust. You should have guards on yourself to stop you from doing that. Not doing their job are they. Naughty guards. You're going to have to watch them guards. You'd better not sleep any more, because if you do, they'll see their chance and slip away again like the sly little rascals they are. Are you ready to stop misbehaving. Are you going to be good, yes. If you're good you can come to our party. We're having a party, aren't we, Lee. What sort of party are we having.

LEE: Poncho party.

MICK: We're having a poncho party. (*He shows LARRY the bottle.*) The rules of a poncho party are, it has to take place on a poncho. Doesn't it Lee. Because that's our magic carpet. Isn't it Lee.

LEE: Yes flying carpet.

MICK: Where shall we fly to, Lee.

LEE: Fly and never land. Wherever you land, all you're going to find is just the force of gravity.

MICK: So are you going to come and have a drink.

LARRY: No.

MICK: Why not.

LARRY: No.

MICK: What's the matter, don't you trust us.

LARRY: No.

MICK: Why don't you trust us.

LARRY: Bureaucrats.

MICK: Are we bureaucrats, are we. I don't think you're all there.

LEE: No it's just. Waking up in a strange bed.

MICK: Is that what it is.

LEE: It's frightening, waking up in a strange bed.

MICK: Well you'd know.

LEE: He just needs to remember where he is.

MICK: Oh yes Lee, that will make him feel so much better.

LEE: Anyway I hope he's ashamed.

MICK: I think he is ashamed, Lee, I think he's got a guilty conscience.

LEE: I hope he has.

MICK: (*To LARRY.*) Some would say death's no more than you deserve.

LEE: Some would say death's too good for him.

MICK: We've always thought America was so great.

LEE: I've always thought America is. Bugs Bunny.

MICK: You'd have shot us down last night as if we'd been just anyone.

LEE: As if we'd been just foreign.

MICK: Pretending not to know us.

LEE: Pretending not to know your own kind.

MICK: There's blokes out there, they'd hang you if they knew what you are.

LEE: You should be glad it's us mate.

MICK: But we're not vengeful, are we Lee.

LEE: No.

MICK: Because that would be childish.

LEE: Childish.

MICK: Because who knows what your reasoning is.

LEE: No-one.

MICK: So fuck it, have a drink.

LARRY: I'm dead.

MICK: We're not going to hurt you.

LARRY: I can see it now, I can see the hand of the bureaucrats in this.

MICK: What do you mean, bureaucrats.

LARRY: The bureaucrats are in favour of England. They govern America, but they are not American. I'm an American, and I say I'll fight who I want, where I want. The bureaucrats are not in favour of that.

MICK: They're after you, are they.

LARRY: Because England is the birthplace of bureaucracy.

MICK: Are they after you then.

LARRY: Top people.

MICK: Top people, are they.

LARRY: In America. In England. They'll be working on this together.

MICK: Thatcher's after you, is she.

LARRY: She's a bureaucrat.

MICK: They all want to kill you do they.

LARRY: I think so. Because the American people would take a dislike to this situation. They would take a dislike to English soldiers fighting against an American boy. They would criticize the bureaucratic obsession with England, and this is what the bureaucrats will be working to prevent. Sure, I'm crazy. Sure.

MICK: I never said that.

LARRY: Do you even know why you're here.

MICK: To safeguard the sovereignty of British people.

LARRY: Antarctica is the reason you're here. This is the point from which England intends to claim a piece of Antarctica. Antarctica. The icebox of the world, full of fish, full of phosphates, and the ground there is all composed of jewels and precious metals and oil, everything man needs is there under the snow just waiting to be uncovered. One of these days they're going to thaw it out with mirrors, and people there will make their homes in bubbles.

MICK: Bubbles eh. Beautiful bubbles.

LARRY: See people say they're doing one thing, but the big thing is happening beyond their conscious mind, you look down one day, you find a new continent has risen up under your feet.

LEE: There's this pool there you can swim in.

LARRY: What pool? Where?

LEE: There's this warm pool. In Antarctica.

MICK: This jacuzzi is there Lee.

LARRY: You mean there's a geyser.

LEE: No, there's no people, no. Oh. A geyser. Yeah. There's a geyser. In a pool.

LARRY: That would be neat. Swimming in that pool with ice all around. That would be neat.

LEE: Yeah. I'm not sure what part it's in.

MICK: Come on, come and have a drink.

LARRY: You guys are only doing what you have to. I'm sorry to meet like this. But guys, if there was some way you could see my way out of this, I sure would appreciate it.

MICK: What's he talking about.

LARRY: Please.

MICK: Come and have a drink.

LARRY: Bring me a drink over here.

MICK: No, you come over to us mate.

LARRY: Why can't I have it here.

MICK: Don't you trust us.

LARRY: Bring it to me here and I'll trust you.

MICK: No you insulted us now. I'm not giving you no drink if you don't trust me.

LARRY: Fuck your drink then.

LEE: Fuck you and all. You can fucking stay there and rot.

MICK: Wait a minute Lee.

LEE: I wouldn't take a drink with him if he asked me.

MICK: Lee.

LEE: Won't take a fucking drink with us, well fuck him.

MICK: Lee. He's frightened Lee. He had a frightening dream. We don't want him feeling frightened Lee.

LEE: Frightened of his own fucking shadow.

MICK: (*To LARRY.*) Are you coming over here then?

LARRY: No.

MICK: We're going to have to get you out of this. Come on. (*Starts pulling LARRY out of the bed.*)

LEE: Come on.

LARRY: No, fuck you, no!

LEE: He's bringing the whole fucking bed with him.

LARRY: No!

LEE: Get his fingers loose.

MICK: (*Trying to undo LARRY's fingers.*) Be reasonable, you're being hysterical, be reasonable.

ADAM enters and stands watching.

LEE: (*To ADAM.*) He won't take a drink with us.

MICK: He's refusing to take a drink.

ADAM: (*To LARRY.*) Don't you want a drink?

LARRY: Give it to me here.

ADAM: Why won't you give it him there.

LEE: Eh.

ADAM: Give him a drink. Give it him there.

LEE: But you said –

ADAM: Give it him there. (*They give LARRY the bottle. LARRY doesn't drink.*) You might as well. Pity to waste it.

LARRY: Sure. (*LARRY drinks.*)

ADAM: Bring him over.

LARRY screams. MICK and LEE drag LARRY over on to the poncho and ADAM kills him with his bayonet.

Cover him. (*They cover him.*)

LEE: (*To ADAM.*) Only you said. He has to be on the poncho. That's what you said. We were doing every fucking thing to get him on the poncho. Then you walk in. Give it him there. We might just as well have saved ourselves the trouble. Give it him there.

ADAM: Shut up Finch.

LEE: But you said –

TOBY enters.

TOBY: I thought I heard a noise.

ADAM: What noise.

TOBY: I thought I heard a noise. (*Silence.*) Have you tried getting through to him.

ADAM: Yes I have sarge.

TOBY: You haven't got through to him then.

ADAM: Yes I have sarge.

TOBY: When did you get through to him.

ADAM: Just now.

TOBY: You didn't tell me.

ADAM: The order's been confirmed sarge.

TOBY: You didn't tell me.

ADAM: He said to get on with it sarge.

TOBY: I don't understand why you couldn't come and tell me.

ADAM: He said to get on with it.

TOBY: All the more reason. All the more reason, corporal. They want us to get on with it, why aren't we getting on with it. It's these problems of communication, corporal.

ADAM: Yes sarge.

TOBY: Once again, these problems of communication.

ADAM: Yes sarge.

TOBY: Who'd have believed it, eh.

ADAM: I believe it, sarge.

TOBY: I never could have believed it. Is it possible.

ADAM: Yes sarge.

TOBY: Is it possible.

ADAM: Would you like to check with him sarge.

TOBY: No, that's all right corporal. Is it possible. Yes it is.
    Well. Anything's possible. Only in practice, you rely on
    certain things not happening, don't you, even if they're
    possible, you rely on certain things not happening. How
    wrong can you be.

ADAM: This isn't one of those things though, is it sarge.

TOBY: I bet that little twat never even asked anyone.

ADAM: Your senior officer, sarge.

TOBY: Or if he did. He asked someone who thought the
    same as him.

ADAM: Most people would think the same as him, sarge.

TOBY: No, most people are not like you lot.

ADAM: Yes. They are. And the proof of it is, they recruited us.

TOBY: But it's wrong. You know it's wrong. Everyone
    knows it's wrong.

ADAM: They know it's wrong sarge, but they want it done.
    There are times when wrong things have to be done.

TOBY: So they don't care.

ADAM: No sarge.

TOBY: Well then. If they don't care. Why should I.

ADAM: That's right sarge.

TOBY: If the law, for which you and I are fighting, corporal, means nothing to them that have the power, then what is this golden banner I've been carrying around. This banner above my head, this pride. What's this banner I've got left on my hands, perishing in my hands, it's just an old thin piece of cloth which I'm carrying for God knows what reason any more.

They have their daylight voice, they have their golden voice. But they also have their night voice, and in the daylight hours they pretend it isn't theirs, even to themselves.

Get him up, take him outside.

ADAM: Eh.

TOBY: Wake him up.

LEE: But sarge.

TOBY: Wake him up, take him outside.

LEE: But sarge, he's –

ADAM: We can do it in his sleep sarge.

TOBY: Now. You mean now.

ADAM: I'll do it. I'll do it sarge.

TOBY: Where's your bayonet.

ADAM: I'll do it.

TOBY: Give it here.

ADAM: Sarge. Are you sure you want to do this.

TOBY: Show me up would you. Give it here.

ADAM: (*Giving him the bayonet.*) In his eye sarge.

TOBY: Don't fucking tell me what to do. I know what to do.

ADAM: Straight in his eye, then you know it's done.

TOBY: What I happen to think of it doesn't matter.

ADAM: You can do it sarge.

TOBY: Do it. Course I can do it.

ADAM: What we all joined up for, isn't it sarge.

TOBY: Course I can do it.

ADAM: Come on sarge, give him a good one.

TOBY: Frankly I don't think much of it. I don't think it's any great achievement frankly.

ADAM: Are you all right, sarge.

TOBY: I don't think it amounts to very much at all. Perfect myself. That's what I wanted. Mentally and physically. Perfect myself. What must they think of us. That twat won't even want to know me after I've done this job. In giving me this job, he reveals how little they think of me. Whenever he sets eyes on me, he'll remember. And he'll say to himself yes, he really is the garbage I thought he was, he proved himself fit for the job.

ADAM: Give it here.

TOBY: Fuck off.

ADAM: Give it here.

TOBY: No wait. No listen. Wait.

ADAM: Give it here.

TOBY: If this is how low they are. They're not worth it.

ADAM: Oh you cunt.

TOBY: No listen. If we can't be proud of what we do, then where's our motivation.

ADAM: I'm proud, you cunt.

TOBY: Why.

ADAM: Because I exist. I'm proud because I exist, and I exist because I'm proud.

TOBY: But you can't be proud if you do things that make you ashamed.

ADAM: That's why I'm never ashamed of what I do.

TOBY: But you should be. They're asking you to do a shameful thing. Therefore they're not worth it. There's nobody to do it for. We're free. We can enjoy our time on earth. We don't have to harm anyone. Everyone can live.

ADAM: (*In total exasperation.*) I don't think so. I really don't think so.

TOBY: I don't want to harm this man. Even this man is infinitely more valuable to me than nothingness. Even this man, lying there asleep, has the depth and life of a forest.

ADAM: A forest, sarge.

TOBY: Yes, even this man is a forest.

ADAM: Listen sarge I understand the principle, but the principle is there for human beings and this man's not what I would call a human being. This man has no conscience, he doesn't know what it's like to be us. He's a setback to the human race.

TOBY: What gives you the right to say that, corporal.

ADAM: You've got a conscience sarge. You're better than him. So it's all right for you to kill him.

TOBY: What's my conscience worth if I don't follow what it says. See, in this engagement, corporal. Already in this engagement the decency is slipping away. Just for the sake of getting on with it. But it slips away so fast, and then it's gone, and everyone's left crawling in the mud not knowing why. Look at him sleeping. (*He looks at LARRY more closely, pulls back the poncho covering him.*) What have you done.

ADAM: Who's asking me.

TOBY: What have you done.

ADAM: Who's asking me. You cunt.

SANDRA enters. TOBY hastily covers LARRY.

SANDRA: (*To ADAM.*) Remember me?

ADAM: Eh.

SANDRA: I'm still down the hall.

ADAM: I know.

SANDRA: Just down there.

ADAM: I know you are.

SANDRA: Are you coming.

ADAM: In a minute.

SANDRA: You do what you want. What's it to me what you do.

TOBY: Go out of here will you love.

SANDRA: I beg your pardon. I beg your pardon.

TOBY: Go on, bugger off out of it.

SANDRA: What's the matter with you? (*To ADAM.*) What's the matter with him?

ADAM: I wish I knew.

TOBY: (*To SANDRA.*) I'm warning you.

SANDRA: (*To TOBY.*) What's your game?

TOBY: For your own sake I'm warning you.

SANDRA: What's happened? (*Registers LARRY.*) He's dead.

ADAM: Well done sarge.

TOBY: She can see for herself.

ADAM: Well done.

TOBY: Can't you love.

SANDRA: Oh my God.

ADAM: (*To SANDRA.*) He shouldn't have told you.

SANDRA: How do you mean, he shouldn't. How do you mean.

Pause.

ADAM: Don't be upset.

SANDRA: Stay away from me.

ADAM: Don't be upset. I'm not going to hurt you. What you take us for.

SANDRA screams.

SANDRA: Stay away from me.

Pause.

ADAM: He's got no business upsetting you like this.

SANDRA: What are you going to do.

ADAM: All that happened, Sandra...

MICK: He tried to escape.

TOBY: Eh.

ADAM: He tried to escape.

Pause.

TOBY: This is it, Sandra, he tried to escape.

ADAM: He was dangerous.

SANDRA: Yes.

TOBY: A dangerous man.

SANDRA: Why did you bring him into my house. Why did you bring him into my house.

TOBY: I never brought him into your house. I'm not the one.

ADAM: No he's not the one, he's never the one, he's never ever been the fucking one! He calls himself my sergeant, and not one fucking thing has he ever done, oh no, he leaves it all up to me, he leaves it all up to anyone who actually cares what actually happens! I can't look to him! Can I! I might as well be looking at a black room through a broken window! What am I supposed to be? I'm only human! I never wanted this! He says to me, special treatment. This man's to have special fucking treatment...

SANDRA: (*To TOBY.*) Now see what you've done! Are you satisfied? You –

TOBY: A hypothetical question Sandra. Just a hypothetical question. Just so I know your opinion. A British platoon captures an American mercenary. What are we supposed to do with him.

ADAM: Oh yes give him special treatment.

TOBY: He's an embarrassment. What are we supposed to do with him?

ADAM: (*To SANDRA.*) Come out of here.

SANDRA: Yes.

TOBY: They want it kept quiet. They don't want it known.

ADAM: Come on.

SANDRA: Yes.

TOBY: How far should they go?

SANDRA: This is a hypothetical question you're asking me.

TOBY: What's it worth to them to keep it quiet? Is it worth his life?

SANDRA: Yes but this is not happening.

TOBY: What's his life worth?

SANDRA: (*To ADAM.*) It's a hypothetical question he's asking me.

TOBY: They'd be making us murderers, wouldn't they. We're not murderers, we're citizens. What are they putting us on the level of. Creatures of the dark. We hate the dark. We're afraid of the dark. We want to live in the light with everyone else.

SANDRA: This isn't a true question he's asking me.

ADAM: No it's not a true question. How could he ask you that question unless it wasn't true. Because if it were true, that would have to be a decision made by very senior people. Very senior people would have decided to keep this man's existence quiet. They would be wanting to keep his existence quiet, so as not to jeopardize the special relationship between England and America, a relationship which is very important to us in this conflict, which is a very difficult and dangerous one. Now Sandra. If this man's existence was having to be kept quiet, then his death would also have to be kept quiet, wouldn't it. Anyone who knew about his death would have to keep it quiet. Wouldn't they.

SANDRA: But none of this is true.

ADAM: No.

SANDRA: What he said isn't true.

ADAM: Some people here, Sandra, have trouble facing up to the reality. There are some people wandering away from the reality, physically and also in their minds, they wander in their minds. Don't they sarge.

TOBY: This is it, Sandra, I think I must be wandering in my mind. Because I'm sane. And all of you are mad. So what does that make me.

ADAM: (*To SANDRA.*) Come on.

SANDRA: Yes.

TOBY: Don't listen to me. Whatever you do. Don't listen to me.

SANDRA: (*To ADAM.*) He frightens me. I'm frightened of him.

ADAM: (*To SANDRA.*) Come on down the hall. (*ADAM and SANDRA off.*)

MICK: (*To TOBY.*) What the fuck's got into you.

TOBY: Who are you speaking to, Pike.

MICK: You'll get us all destroyed. Will you be happy then. Will you finally be happy.

TOBY: Who are you speaking to.

MICK: What's the point of trying to tell her anyway, she doesn't want to know. Nor should she! It's a specialized matter. For specialists.

TOBY: Am I mad?

MICK: Who cares if you're mad, do the job, that's all, do the fucking job.

LEE: Yes but Mick.

TOBY: Am I mad.

LEE: What is the job.

MICK: Do the job.

LEE: What is the job.

MICK: (*To LEE.*) Don't you start.

LEE: (*To MICK.*) I always want to be proud of what I've done.

MICK: Who's stopping you.

LEE: Yes but I'm not.

MICK: Have a drink sarge, put your thoughts in order. (*He retrieves his bottle of whisky from the floor.*)

LEE: I'm not.

MICK: Cheer up sarge. (*Offering the bottle to TOBY, who takes no notice.*) Have a drink.

TOBY: The moment she appeared.

MICK: Who sarge.

MICK and LEE start wrapping LARRY's body.

TOBY: Press the button just as she came round the corner then stand to attention.

LEE: Are you all right sarge.

TOBY: Soon as the doors were open I had to slip inside the lift and hold down the Door Open button.

MICK: Did you sarge did you really.

TOBY: Once she was safely in, I had to stand outside saluting while the doors closed. Then I had to run like buggery up three flights of stairs, and be stood there at attention and not out of breath ready to salute her when the lift arrived...

LEE: Brilliant eh sarge.

TOBY: I trained three weeks for that.

MICK: Nobody does it like we do sarge.

LEE: Brilliant eh.

THE END